The Phoenix Factor:

How to be an indispensable contributor in a post-pandemic world.

Donald J. Minnick, PhD

Lessons from a pandemic:

While our worlds have become more remote, our need for connection and involvement is more urgent. Success has a new meaning: developing as an individual to your highest potential and helping others to succeed and thrive as a result of leveraging your talent and optimizing your luck.

> *"I look upon us as partners in all of this, and that each of us contributes and does what he can do best. And so, I see not a top rung and a bottom rung - I see all this horizontally - and I see this as part of a matrix. And I see every human being as having a purpose, a destiny, if you like - the destiny to make a difference in the world."*

> — Jonas Salk

CONTENTS

Preface

The World Has Changed… So Has the Workplace… and So Have We…

The handwriting is on the wall and all over the news. Headlines tell the story:

> *'Global Layoffs Pile Up As Recession Woes Mount: Scientists say it's too soon to predict how the pandemic will end'* - CBS News

> *'Nothing Compares: Over 1.18 Million Americas Filed for Unemployment Last Week'* - Associated Press

> *'Pandemic and Economic Instability Wrecks Global Class of 2020's Hopes for First Job'* - ABC News

> *'Pandemic Plateaus Hiring, Hurts Skilled Workers'* - MSN Business

> *'Reimagining the Post-Pandemic Organization Takes Us in Completely New Directions'* - McKinsey Quarterly

> *'Small Businesses Devastated by Covid-19'* - Reuters Business

This is nothing particularly new. Economic cycles come and go. Businesses pull back when times are lean, then invest aggressively when money is abundant and new opportunities arise. But this seems different. This is beyond the natural economic cycles of boom and bust.

Sure, the face of business was changing anyway: more independence; a gig economy; remote work. But then came *Covid-19* and, at least for a time, it shut the world down. Suddenly, and for an extended period of time we were forced to consider what 'business' would look like post-pandemic (if there is a 'post pandemic' - some medical experts predict that this is just the first of many global pandemics to come).

When businesses inevitably change, the question becomes:

How can we, as individuals, contribute in ways that make us indispensable AND help our company survive?

How do we bounce back? We don't. *We bounce **forward** !*

Introduction

Co-Evolution: How Businesses and Individuals Were Transformed

"There is nothing more difficult to take in hand, more perilous to conduct, or more uncertain in its success than to take the lead in the introduction of a new order of things."

- Jean- Jacques Rousseau

Co-evolution, a concept borrowed from the field of biology, refers to the changes among interdependent systems such that their evolutionary paths become intertwined over time. As systems adapt to their larger environment, they also adapt to one another. This interdependence results in each system helping the other to survive in the larger environment, especially in times of change or crisis.

The concept of co-evolution accurately described the changes that had taken place in the structure of American companies over the last 50 years, and the corresponding changes in how individual employees were rewarded and achieved success within those organizations. Those factors that shaped the American business enterprise during that time period include:

Globalization of the economy
- Diversification of the workforce
- Customer-driven economies
- Technological and innovative change

A global pandemic added some new wrinkles and some new business imperatives.

- **Inertia is clearly riskier than action right now**. Companies are mobilizing to address the immediate threat in ways they may have struggled with when taking on more abstract challenges, such as digital technology, automation, and artificial intelligence. Bold experiments and new ways of working are now everyone's business.
- **Businesses must take a stand on 'purpose'**. If the pandemic is teaching us anything, it's that people and

organizations are interconnected and responsible to one another and to society in ways beyond short-term earnings.

- **Companies are reimagining how they create value**. What is an 'essential' business has taken on new meaning and caused us to reflect on what's important in our lives.
- **Getting intentional about organizational culture has become critical**. It may seem invisible during prosperous times, but in moments of crisis, company culture can be seen clearly in the collective behaviors that either help a business pull together and get things done or lead to inertia, confusion, and even mistrust.
- **Striking the appropriate balance between supportive and challenging leadership**. Encouraging people to step up and lead in new ways and seize personal ownership for outcomes is a pure survival strategy.
- **Moving beyond a 'hierarchy of bosses' toward more agile working structures.** Encouraging a high degree of autonomy for people closest to customers, partners, and community contributes to effective decision-making, innovation, and getting things done.
- **Fostering a high degree of alignment across groups so that the right things get done in the first place.** What has always stood in the way of these aims is a reflexive, single-minded adherence to hierarchy in its many guises: organization charts, solid and dotted-line reporting, and spans of control.
- **Turbocharge decision making**. Making good decisions faster - and with imperfect information is the agility required in the new world of work.
- **Treat talent as your scarcest resource**. Everything else: technology, access to raw materials, intellectual property, and customer relationships is fleeting. The only sustainable advantage is rooted in harnessing the passion, skills, capabilities, judgment, and creativity that people bring to work every day.
- **Adopt an eco-system talent mindset.** One such opportunity will be increased access to new talent pools as a result of remote working. Being able to tap into global talent has always been a challenge because people had to relocate. This

9

crisis will change that. We'll be able to hire talent from around the world - and they won't have to relocate.

- **Learn how to learn**. The working world after the pandemic will be different, companies will be different, and many people will themselves be different as a result of their experiences during the crisis. Organizations that equip their employees with the meta-skill of learning how to learn, adapt, and change quickly will be better able to thrive and to succeed.

- **Business model resilience**. A sustainable, flexible and a portfolio-based approach to work strategy must be at the heart. The longstanding focus on efficiency and growth in the workplace will likely give way to one of business-model resilience. This is because we have seen how volatile the world is and we now appreciate the numerous potential discontinuities out there.

What do we know about what the 'new company' will look like? Nik Kinley with *YSC Consulting* [1] has worked to capture and sharpen these distinctions. He teamed with *IMD Business School* to research crises and recessions of the past 100 years to see what could be learned about what businesses need to do now. He studied acute crises such as 9/11 and Hurricane Katrina, as well as more prolonged recessions such as the Great Depression of the 1930's and the 2008 financial crisis.

Here's what he discovered. *'Businesses are in the grip of an unprecedented health social and economic crisis. For some it has brought unusually heavy demand and with it an extraordinary opportunity for growth. But for most it has brought a sudden stop or abrupt change and with it much pain and challenge. Employees are dispersed, supply chains disrupted, customers disappeared. Simple survival or the implementation of some sort of continuity plan was step one. But while that may be a win in its own right, it's not enough and the key question facing many businesses now is what to do next as either the recession elongates or recovery comes'.*

He discovered that during previous crises around 17% of firms effectively collapse, and around 75% struggle but survive. About 9% percent of companies undergoing major crises seem to thrive, significantly outperforming competitors. In fact, how businesses perform during the crisis is more important than pre-crisis performance, business size or age.

Kinley found three specific business behaviors that are most commonly seen in the businesses that thrive.
- **Efficiency**: a focus not just on cash and costs, but on operational efficiency - or using the crisis to make their businesses 'fitter'.
- **Evolution**: output-side investment in things like product development and marketing.
- **Empowerment:** businesses that are decentralized and empower employees did better. The positive effect of this is primarily driven through creating local discretion over outputs - sales and new products, rather than inputs like labor and capital.

This book takes up the question: *'How do we as individuals need to adapt to survive this crisis in the working world and how can we best make a contribution to our company going forward'?*

We're not just building a career any longer, our imperative has become more about contribution - just as we had to focus on how we could help each other survive during the pandemic.

What *Covid-19* has taught us:

- **The demands on our attention have decreased**. Multi-tasking is not so important. Now our job is to learn, absorb and interact in mindful ways, taking notice of our thoughts and habits.
- **We can allow our minds to dictate our judgments and decisions**. Rather than being directed exclusively by the external world, we have opportunity to be especially attentive. We can break free of the habits that have dictated our actions and try for something else. We can stop going through our days in a mindless haze. How many ideas and insights have escaped because you forgot to pay attention? How many decisions or judgments have you made without realizing how or why you made them - driven by some

internal default settings whose existence you're only vaguely aware of. How many days have gone by where you suddenly wonder exactly what you did and how you got to where you are? Now we can build habits of thought that will allow us to engage mindfully with ourselves and with the world as a matter of choice.

- **Our brains are extraordinarily adept at learning new ways of thinking**. Our neural connections are remarkably flexible, even as we continue to age.
- **We can adopt a natural skepticism and inquisitiveness toward the world**. In this new world nothing is taken at face value, everything is scrutinized and considered and only then accepted - or not.

As this book goes forward we will elaborate a set of broad adaptive behaviors that describe the best fit for individual success and contribution within the new world of business:

- An inclination towards proactivity and personal initiative
- A talent for collaboration with others
- An ability to deal with change creatively
- Being seen by others as competent and influential
- Having a broad-based knowledge of the workings of the organization
- An ability to work effectively in team environments
- Capacity to leverage the unexpected – both the good and bad luck that comes your way

Why A Phoenix?

Change is happening everywhere we look. Unique, creative solutions are emerging before our eyes. The challenge facing leaders across the world is two-fold:

- How to nurture and drive the right positive actions to break out of the chaotic space.
- How to sense innovative solutions as they emerge so organizations can grasp and build upon those ideas.

It takes a wise leader to know when to change something. It takes insight to recognize when it's time for transformation. There are multiple stories in various mythologies about the creation of order out of chaos. We have chosen the *Phoenix*.

The phoenix is best known as a being of Greek mythology, but it has analogs in many other traditions and is almost culturally universal: including the Hindu *Garuda*; The Russian firebird *Zhar-ptitsa*; the Persian *Simurgh*; the Georgian *Paskunji*; the Arabian *Anga*; the Turkish *Konrul*; the Tibetan *Me byi karmo*; the Chinese *Fenghuang*; and in Japan the mythical Phoenix was adopted as a symbol of the imperial household, particularly the Empress. The Phoenix myth is also part of early Christian traditions as an allegory for the resurrection of Christ.

The story of the Phoenix is legendary and is likely one of the most well-known ancient myths in modern day. The legend is famous for the many elements it is said to concern - life and death, creation and destruction, even time itself is tied with the tale of the Phoenix.

The Phoenix was known to be a majestic bird-like creature that lived in *Paradise*. However, in time, the bird began to feel the effects of its age. After 1,000 years had passed, it was ready to move on. As the Phoenix was known to live in *Paradise*, it was also known that it could never truly die. It rose from the ashes of its own destruction. Creation from chaos.

So how does the symbol of the Phoenix fit our current post-pandemic world?

It's more important now than ever before that we move towards what is desirable and not just go to our defaults. There is an element of 'sense-breaking' so we can move to 'sense-making' that better fits our new world. We must be transforming. Systems designed for ordinary times are not suited to extraordinary times. One of the most important things is to build systems that allow us to capture lessons learned. We need situational assessment so that we can increase the cognitive/experiential diversity in the way people make decisions. We connect around our similarities and benefit from our differences.

All these various elements of our *Phoenix Factor Model* will be further elaborated in this book in due course.

What Our Collective History Teaches Us: Our Heroes Define Our Culture

Much of the stories involving the Plymouth Plantation, Benjamin Franklin, the Lewis and Clark expedition and Dale Carnegie were drawn from Jay Parini's wonderful 2008 book: *Promised Land: thirteen books that changed America.*[2] These stories give vibrant examples of the skills that are outlined later in this book.

In the United States where failure is shameful and success has become something of a religion, the roots of what it takes to survive, and in fact thrive in challenging times go as deep as the history of the country. How do people respond when placed in uncertain situations, with incomplete information? History has some answers.

The stories of those men and women in our collective past that we most admire, and their exploits, laid the groundwork for the proud American tradition of survival against the odds - and the foundations of the concepts of 'contribution' which I was to discover in more detail much later through my consulting work.

These four pioneering stories (among many others) can teach us not only how to survive, but how to thrive and indeed change the world. The post-*Covid-19* mentality will occupy a place in history with all these previous greats - world changers.

What do they have to teach us? Read these stories with a foreshadowing of the skills we will examine in more detail later in this book.

<u>The Plymouth Plantation</u>: *(Think: Initiative, Collaboration, and a Social Contract to help one another)*

The pilgrims of the *Plymouth Plantation* - one hundred twenty hardy souls: men, women, and children, set out on September 6, 1620, from their homes in northern England via the Netherlands on the *Mayflower* for the freedom and opportunity they hoped to find in the new world. The pilgrims originally set off in two ships the larger being the famous *Mayflower*. The smaller ship was the *Speedwell* which proved hopelessly leaky and was quickly forced to return to England. It was necessary to reduce the size of the group. Twenty or so were left behind, the rest crowding onto the *Mayflower*. Many on the ship were strangers. The reason for risking their lives in the new world was largely financial. Like so many immigrants over the centuries, they set off for the Americas to make their fortune. This was America's first integration narrative. They endured unbelievable hardship, including a harrowing 65-day trip across the Atlantic. The ship was nearly overwhelmed at points by storm-driven seas. Moreover, sanitary conditions were such that infections and diseases spread rapidly and a number of passengers succumbed, their bodies tossed overboard.

Once they arrived, the Pilgrims faced disease and starvation. Nearly half of the entire colony died within the first three months. They survived that difficult first year with help from the local indigenous people. The *Massasoit* nation provided crucial survival skills as well as much needed supplies. By the end of February barely 50 Pilgrims remained with many ill or weak. Most of the women and children had died and less than half of the original 26 men survived. Nevertheless, they persevered. The first Thanksgiving was a traditional harvest festival attended by 90 of the local native Americans. The party lasted three days. The great store of wild turkeys eaten by the revelers is the basis for our current habit in the United States of eating turkeys on Thanksgiving. Abraham Lincoln later seized on the story of the *Plymouth Plantation*, deciding in 1863, in the depths of the Civil War, that Thanksgiving should become a national holiday with its myth of survival through cooperation and mutual respect.

The *Plymouth Plantation* succeeded in part because the colonists took their social compact seriously. They shared resources fairly and worked for the common good, pulling together for the benefit of the community. The famous *Mayflower Compact* was essentially a signed agreement to band together for the mutual safety and well-being of the group, creating a civil body politic. In this brief document we see the shadowy beginnings of the American experiment in democracy.

Calvin Coolidge would later say, *'The business of America is business'*, and this was certainly true of the original pilgrims. The Plymouth colony did more than survive, they thrived. They began to trade in beaver and otter skins, among other commodities. In their systematic experiments in communal living, they parceled out land in a way that would have stirred the heart of Karl Marx, with each family getting a plot commensurate with its size. This anxiety about communal living has rippled through American society since, as its citizens ponder the degree to which they should band together for the common good - or not. Americans sometimes still resist sharing the wealth, except in the form of voluntary charities. There is a deep-seated feeling that one should work only for one's self interest without regard for the larger group. Yet this is only *one* strain in our national discourse. A consistent push from the communal side appears throughout our history. There is testimony from the various well-known experiments in utopian living that became prominent in the 19th century - including the *Harmonists*, the *Shakers* and the *Perfectionists* of the *Oneida's Colony*. In a sense this experiment was reborn in countless hippie communes of the late 1960s and 1970s.

The story of the Plymouth Pilgrims is a story of a people who chose to make their own way in the world, however difficult it might prove to be, and who succeeded.

Benjamin Franklin: *(Think: Proactivity, Action Learning, Personal Visibility and Boundary Spanning)*

Benjamin Franklin's story is the quintessential American success story of a boy without the benefits of family connections, without formal education or inherited wealth rising through the ranks of colonial society to a position of wealth and influence. His rise was self-directed - the product of hard work and ingenuity. Franklin put himself forward in the world through his industriousness and his diligence. He quickly became the most valuable person in a small printing shop in Philadelphia where he initially found work after he had run away from his home in Boston at the age of 17. He fortified his position by every means available until he had made himself indispensable. He had a gregarious nature and attracted a circle of like-minded friends - a company of young men on the make much like himself. He applied himself to any task at hand with an aggressive self-discipline, rising early and working late. More importantly he used his remarkable social skills to continue to build his ever-expanding network of acquaintances and business associates. His circle of friends grew impressively wider as the decades passed and there was often a major patron, someone of considerable wealth or position, who spotted the talents of this young man and pushed him forward in the world.

Among the founding fathers, Franklin presents the most accessible figure by far. Washington and Jefferson seemed titans by comparison, but all but unapproachable.

We have all met Franklin a thousand times in the shops or offices along Main Street - the young man on the move, sweetly affable and eager to please, a bit wily perhaps, but always ready to pitch in. Young Ben eagerly organized his fellow shopkeepers and merchants into groups to discuss interesting topics and promote the public good

At the ripe old age of 22, he quickly established himself as one of the most formidable of printers in the colonies, successful as both printer and publisher, eventually buying the fledgling newspaper *The Pennsylvania Gazette.*

His sayings, printed over the years in the famous *Poor Richard's Almanac,* published in 1732 at the age of 26, helped shape the American character and remain part of our mental fabric: *'Haste makes waste'; 'Little strokes fell great oaks'; 'Fish and visitors stink in three days'.* He believed his Puritan roots that *'God helps those that help themselves'.* He didn't invent many of these sayings, but what he did was polish the old sayings and made them memorable,

17

giving them a local accent, all in keeping with the tradition of aphorisms which are just clever sayings that go around and around. Franklin was so witty, talkative and convincing that Americans tend to think he said things that more or less sound like him. He published his famous *Thirteen Virtues*: Temperance, Silence, Order, Resolution, Frugality, Industry, Sincerity, Justice, Moderation, Cleanliness, Tranquility, Chastity, Humility. Franklin planned to give a week's strict attention to each of the virtues. The idea was to master each virtue by concentrating on it exclusively for a week at a time, much as tennis players might concentrate on footwork or a particular shot in perfecting their game.

Although Franklin lacked a formal education, he had an intense desire to learn about the world. Apparently, nothing fell beyond his curiosity and he never worried about being an expert before attempting an experiment or pursuing a line of inquiry. Anything and everything absorbed Benjamin Franklin and he moved through the world with staggering self-confidence, willing to take risks and even to make a fool of himself

Among his achievements, he established a city watch - in effect a Police Department. He started a company for the 'ready extinguishing of fires' - a volunteer fire department, and he came up with the idea of fire insurance. Observing the lack of a college for advanced studies, he drew up a proposal for establishing an Academy, that evolved into the *University of Pennsylvania*. He erected a public hospital for the cure of impoverished sick persons. He founded the first subscription library on American soil. He served as postmaster of Philadelphia.

In his later years, he became focused on experiments. He stayed close to the surface of life tinkering with gadgets improving everything around him as well as he could. Among his many inventions - the Franklin stove - a clean burning device that improved the lives of householders in colonial America. He refused to take out a patent on the stove although one was offered. It was so with many of his inventions. He felt no desire of profiting by patents himself. The public good came before his personal wealth.

He was a scientist - the man who figured out that lightning was a form of electricity. He famously flew a kite to experiment with a theory. Following on from this discovery he invented the lightning rod. He crafted the first bifocal glasses, one of his most enduring and useful inventions. A printer by profession, he tinkered endlessly with the mechanics of his craft, making improvements in copperplate design. He was interested in magnetism. He seemed always to have been fascinated by medicine where he made numerous innovations and suggestions that have shown him to be stunning and astonishingly prescient.

Franklin's is the story of a young man who put himself bravely forward in the world with shrewd calculation. By thrift and diligence and by constant application to the work of self-perfection, he achieved amazing things. This pattern became, in due course, a model of self-invention and one that would shape a nascent nation's sense of itself as a place where anything was possible if you tried hard enough. This was at its most elementary level the American dream

Lewis and Clark: *(Think: Participant Observation, Creating Collaborative Meaning, and Action Learning)*

At the beginning of the 19th century Merriweather Lewis and William Clark set out on their journey to explore the vast territory recently added to the United States through the *Louisiana Purchase* and to push west to the Pacific in search of a trade route through the northwest that would have inestimable commercial value connecting the United States with the maritime trade on the Pacific. Westward expansion still lay ahead of the nation. Their expedition fired the imagination of many within the 17 states already part of the United States. Through their journey, the eventual shape of the United States began to dawn on Americans who could suddenly imagine what it might mean for the country to own the entire continent - coast to coast.

A secondary goal was to collect scientific information about the region as well as to map it. Geographical understanding was severely limited in 1804. The maps that Clark drew proved invaluable to later explorers. Lewis and Clark did the work of charting the true course of the upper Missouri river and its tributaries. Their measurements of latitude and longitude and their notes on the weather assisted later explorers in their preparations.

President Thomas Jefferson had personally commissioned Captain Lewis, his private secretary, to form the expedition. Lewis was 29 and Clark 33. They were old friends and former comrades. Both were professional soldiers. Clark himself had some experience of the various native American tribes. Lewis was somewhat dreamy by nature, but he fully understood the diplomatic and commercial implications of this journey. Clark was more practical - the sort of man who took control of day-to-day operations negotiating with his men as well as the indigenous natives encountered along the way. Lewis had a mind for the details of botany and zoology and his talent as a naturalist informs the journals they kept. Clark had a better-than-adequate knowledge of geography and topography and he was also a gifted outdoorsman. Both men were skilled with boats. The combination of their talents worked well.

Their journey began in Saint Louis on May 14th, 1804. They took daily notes which they later transferred into bound journals. Their journey eventually covered 8000 miles. They moved along the Missouri River to a winter camp in what is now North Dakota. They continued on through spring, over the continental divide. Along the way they gathered new guides and translators, including Toussaint Charbonneau, a French-Canadian explorer and trader, and his Shoshoni bride Sacagawea. This group of about 40 men and one woman made their way by horseback and canoe down various rivers to the mouth of the Columbia river on the Pacific coast. Their expedition lasted almost two and a half years, taking them through territories rarely if ever seen by white men before. On November 7th, 1805 Clark records a landmark moment for the expedition. *'Great joy in camp. We are now in view of the ocean, this great Pacific.'* After wintering out in what is now Oregon, they returned as heroes to Saint Louis arriving in late September, 1806.

The story of Lewis and Clark is a story about what it means to launch and to do what must be done. The American character itself was affected by the heroic efforts of these adventurers who have thus far inspired two subsequent centuries of explorers, including Neil

Armstrong and Buzz Aldrin, the astronauts who landed their lunar module on the moon in the summer of 1969.

Dale Carnegie: *(Think: Reciprocity, Collaboration and Personal Visibility)*

In America, the myth of self-creation and pulling oneself up by the bootstraps is pervasive, although, its reality is too easily assumed in a world where class, race and gender still present formidable barriers.

It was 1936 - the dark days of the *Great Depression*. Breadlines formed in the streets in cities and towns across the country. Never had failure been so palpable, so vividly on display. Men could no longer occupy the honorable position of 'breadwinner'. Children were hungry. Women felt helpless to support their husbands and their families. Employment was scarce and so the competition for the few precious jobs became cutthroat. Into this ethos came Dale Carnegie's *How to Win Friends and Influence People* (1936) - a cheerful book that turned the heads of millions, giving them a specific way to reinvent themselves in a country where self-invention still defines our culture.

Carnegie taught people how to get ahead by opening up to other people and their concerns. Indeed, at the core of the book Carnegie puts forth the notion of honest appreciation. He taught readers to find something valuable in others and to connect with them for mutual benefit.

Although it was pitched at 'sales' this was not about sales so much as it was about figuring out how to make a contribution. *'Do the thing that you fear to do and the death of fear is absolutely certain'*. As Carnegie tells us, any fool can criticize condemn and complain and most fools do, but it takes character and self-control to be understanding. He had tapped into the deepest principle of human nature - the craving to be recognized and appreciated.

Carnegie rightly understood that we succeed in life by giving up a 'self-only' orientation and by living for the good of others. Of course, this insight lies at the core of Christianity if not most of the world's religions. Likewise, Carnegie suggests that we should lead by example. He tells the story of John Wanamaker, the famous owner of department stores, who one day was walking through one of his large stores and found a customer waiting for service at a counter. Rather than criticize the sales people who were talking in the background, Wanamaker himself got behind the counter and helped the person to purchase an item. He then handed it to the sales people to wrap. Not a word was said in criticism but the point was made. Model what you want to see in others.

Carnegie offers a list of things the reader must do, such as keep a journal of results. Progress he held must be externalized, cataloged and made apparent. It is exhilarating to see abstract principles put into action - practical suggestions. What Carnegie did quite brilliantly was give self-improvement a systematic face.

The takeaway? A proper understanding of human experience entails a complex mix of community interconnectedness. We succeed to the extent that we can help each other succeed.

The achievements of these men and women, along with those of many others, established patterns that have become, in due course, a model that would shape a nation's sense of itself as a place where anything was possible if you used all your talents and tried hard enough: the American dream.

What About Luck?

'Life's single lesson: that there is more accident to it than a man can ever admit to in a lifetime and stay sane'.
— Thomas Pynchon

'It is a great piece of skill to know how to guide your luck even while waiting for it'.
— Baltasar Gracián,
17th century Spanish philosopher

'Fortune is the ruler of half our actions... she allows the other half, or thereabouts to be governed by us'.

- Niccolo Machiavelli

Of course luck matters. Suppose you are an athlete who is committed to hard work, practice and preparation. Right before the big game you trip and break your ankle. None of your planning matters now. Luck is the ultimate insult to human reason. You can't ignore it, yet you can't plan for it. Man's grandest ideas fail if they are hit with bad luck and the most absurd notions can succeed with good luck.

The pandemic has certainly shown us the effect of 'luck'. While it may have been predictable at the macro, policy, and global health agency level, for regular individuals it was a stroke of bad luck none of us anticipated, nor planned for. But here it was nonetheless, impacting our lives in a profound way.

Sir Ronald Aylmer Fisher, a 20th century statistician and geneticist pointed out in 1966: *'The one chance in a million will undoubtedly occur with no less and no more than its appropriate frequency, however surprised we may be that it should occur to us'*. But when one considers the 7.8 billion people who currently make up the world's population, you can be sure that the highly improbable is happening to someone with regular frequency - die of a freak accident; fall ill with a mysterious disease; win the lottery. That 'one chance in a million,' in fact, takes place every second. [3]

Probability - statistics - are as pure as real numbers and a part of life, neither good nor bad. Sometimes we introduce emotion into probability and it becomes 'luck'. Chance that has suddenly acquired a valence, positive or negative - good luck or bad luck. Some of us invest luck with even more meaning, direction, and intent. It becomes fate, karma, kismet, predestination: *'It was meant to be'.*

In the business world, chance can be a merger or acquisition that puts your carefully cultivated career in jeopardy. Or it can be a global pandemic that shuts down or radically alters the business or the locale that you occupy.

There is a tension of these two forces in our lives - luck vs. skill. Anyone can get lucky or unlucky in a single moment. In fact, there is a U-shaped relationship between chance and talent.

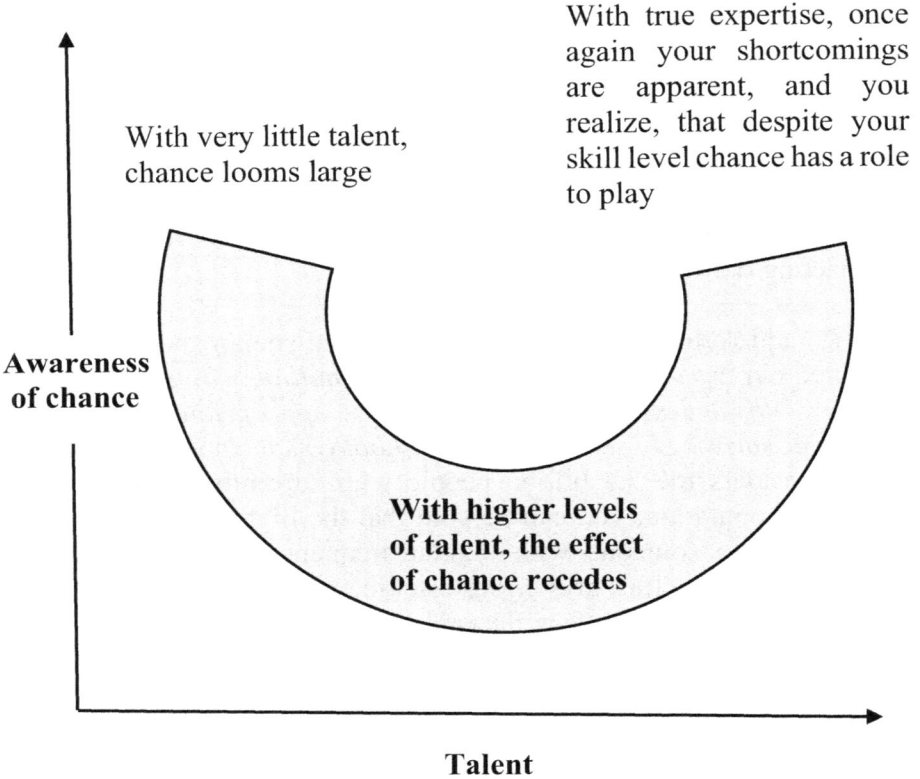

With very little talent, chance looms large

With true expertise, once again your shortcomings are apparent, and you realize, that despite your skill level chance has a role to play

Awareness of chance

With higher levels of talent, the effect of chance recedes

Talent

That's the thing about luck - you do what you can, but in the end some things remain stubbornly outside your control.

The American psychologist Julian Rotter [4] used the terms internal vs. external *locus of control* that seem applicable here. An *internal locus of control* reflects a belief that one can control one's own life, while an *external locus of control* reflects a belief that life is controlled by outside factors - that luck, chance or fate rule our lives.

Of, course you can't control your luck in a very precise way - 'I'll win the lottery tomorrow'. But you can bring about substantial and even startling improvements in the quality of your luck. You can turn it from mostly bad to mostly good and from pretty good to better. Luck happens and through it all we persist - gaining perspective, survival skills, and the strengths and knowledge to be the conqueror and not the conquered. So, we control what we can: our thinking, our decision processes, our reactions. In fact, anyone can get lucky - or unlucky. One turn of luck and you're on top of the world, or you're cast out. In the end, though, luck is a short-term friend or foe. Skill persists.

Skill can open up new vistas, new choices. Skill can allow us to see the chance that others less skilled, less observant, or less keen might miss. But should chance go against us, all our talent can do is mitigate the damage - and that may be just enough to make the difference. Putting in place a systematic learning process of new skills *or* mindfully applying the talents you already possess, helps you unravel chance from everything else.

Fortunately, there is some well-researched writing that addresses the role of luck in our lives and provides information we can use to our advantage.

Maria Konnikova graduated from *Harvard University* and earned her Ph.D. in psychology from *Columbia University*. Her graduate research focused on how people make decisions in uncertain situations with incomplete information. She has written two New York Times bestsellers: *Mastermind: how to think like Sherlock Holmes,* Penguin Books, 2013; and *The Biggest Bluff: how I learned to pay attention, master myself and win,* Penguin Press

2020. While researching the latter book, she learned the game of poker from scratch (she didn't even know how many cards were in a deck) and became an international poker champion.

Journalist and writer Max Gunther was the author of 26 books. He graduated from *Princeton University* and served in the U.S. Army. He had a particular interest in what characteristics distinguished universally acknowledged 'lucky' people from those others considered spectacularly 'unlucky' and he teased out the factors at play. Two of his books capture these findings: *The Luck Factor: why some people are luckier than others and how you can become one of them,* McMillan Publishing Company, 1977; and *How to Get Lucky: 13 techniques for discovering and taking advantage of life's good breaks*, Harriman House Publishers, 1986.

These two researchers and authors teach us that, within limits, but in a perfectly real way, luck can be influenced. Sense can be made of it. It can be handled *rationally*. Gunther's and Konnikova's research shows that lucky people share similar attitudes and behavioral characteristics that allow many apparent random outcomes to be controlled. We'll explore these characteristics in much more detail and build specific skills around them later in the book. But here's a quick preview.

'Lucky' people seem to share four specific characteristics: [5]

1. They mix it up. Lucky people are extroverted and eager to experiment. They embrace new experiences and vary their routines to throw themselves in serendipity's way, increasing their odds of a lucky break.
2. They listen to their gut - not constantly weighing the pros and cons of any decision in ways that can lead to paralysis. They tune into how they *feel* about the decisions in their lives
3. They never quit. Unlucky people collapse under bad luck - lucky people see it as a learning experience.
4. They're broadly and generally optimistic.

Good luck strikes those that are open to it.

Good luck is great to have, but you can also position yourself to take advantage of good luck when it arrives and mitigate the ill-effects of bad luck when it happens. Gunther calls this *'the luck adjustment'*.

So there it is. It's 'talent' + 'luck' that shapes our outcomes. It's good to have both. But if you don't… the good news is that both can be cultivated.

How I Met the 'Key Contributor'

Step into today's world and today's organization. Who are the really indispensable people in this company? When I ask this question of my consulting clients, the answers invariably go something like this:

"When I need to get an important order out the door, I call Lori".

"The best sales manager in the company is Marc, hands down".

"If I need an accurate cost fast, I call Noland, he's amazing".

The same names keep coming up again and again: the high performers, the *'go-to'* individuals. Companies build their businesses around these people. For an organization, that is the key to the gold mine.

While circumstances beyond your control certainly play a role - a flattening economy, company downsizings, mergers, acquisitions, or a global pandemic - making yourself indispensable in your organization, keeping your job and making a contribution in troubled economic times depend more and more on a clear strategy and a specific set of skills. That's what my 30+ years of consulting experience has taught me.

I took a somewhat circuitous route to my eventual focus on who were the organizational movers and shakers. I began my academic career as a math major at a prestigious undergraduate institution. I chose math the same way many of us choose career paths - not because I was particularly interested in the field, but because I was good at it in high school: always straight-A's in math. *'Oh, you're good at math. You should major in that at college.'* However, in college, I soon discovered the sterile, highly cerebral work of theoretical math was not for me.

Meanwhile I began to notice that, over in the psychology department, they were doing some really interesting stuff. In addition, the undergraduates in that department seemed a lot cooler than my nerdy math buddies. I felt that I had found my niche. So, during the second half of my academic career, I was off in pursuit of a doctorate in clinical psychology. However, as I prepared for a traditional clinical practice, I soon learned that I was less interested in the inner workings of the mind and its struggles - especially in the clinically disordered mind - and much more interested in how the individual fit into the systems of family, job, community, and the larger world. I had some training in 'family systems' psychotherapy, and this model had something to say about how an individual adjusts in the larger social setting.

Early in my postdoctoral professional work, I was invited by a former graduate school classmate to serve as a program director for a series of management training programs conducted within a very large Fortune 100 chemical company. The program focused on how individual style played out in the work environment - what aspects of a manager's personal style worked to make the manager more productive, and what aspects of personal style proved to be counterproductive. Much of this work involved listening to and capturing the managers' own experiences and creating 'learnable moments' around this material for the benefit of all the participants in the programs.

Over the last 30 years, I have been engaged in similar organization development work, with areas of focus including: helping managers and individual contributors build interpersonal excellence in their organizations, the study of leadership emergence and its development, and team facilitation and organizational high performance. My clients include a wide spectrum of business and industry from space-related, highly technical, scientific organizations to the energy sector - primarily the oil and gas business, financial service organizations, big pharma, professional service organizations, and consumer goods companies. These businesses range in size from massive Fortune 100 organizations to small entrepreneurial start-ups. What I discovered was that in every industry, although the problems and the focus of the business differ somewhat, the human element is remarkably similar. The questions that arise for the individuals in these companies include:

- "How do I mobilize my best efforts to contribute to the organization's cause"?
- "How can I be a valuable member to my team"?
- "How can I build my skills so that I stay on top of my industry and remain prepared for any challenge"?
- "How can I be seen as competent and a valuable organization member by my peers"?
- "How can I impress those up the chain of command and document my value"?

A few years ago, during a previous period of economic recession, my colleagues and I at *Interpersonal Skills Laboratory, LLC,* began to collect data - with the help of our consulting clients - which ultimately became the model you're are about to discover. At first, we simply listened to our clients while they discussed the skills that seemed to contribute to their own and to others' value to the organization. Later, we embarked on a path to build a model for framing these new success skills. We wanted to get a clear bead on what specific skills add to an individual's ability to be an essential contributor. Our hunch was that these individual skills not only made employees indispensable, but these same skills contributed to the success of the entire organization as well. Over the last ten years, we have collected survey data from several hundred individuals within our client systems. These were all individuals who were squarely in the midst of the evolving organization and the rapidly changing business climate.

In our surveys we posed these questions:

- "List the personal characteristics, skills, or competencies of those employees who will be most valuable to your organization".
- "If you are a manager who selected employees to staff your

29

evolving company, what specific skills did you look for"?

- "Give a specific example of a behavior that is most characteristic of an employee - with whom you have had personal experience - who you believe is *indispensable*".

As the results came in, three surprising factors stood out. First, almost no one referenced technical skills. It seemed to be understood by our respondents that the technical ability to do a job well was a given - technical skill alone was no longer a distinguishing factor. Second, although the skills that were identified seemed to come more naturally to some, they were certainly within the range of learnable skills for everyone. Finally, certain elements seemed to represent part of an underlying nature: an orientation toward people, an inclination toward action, or a willingness to take the lead, for example. Other elements seemed to describe more specific (and learnable) skillsets: a creative approach to problem solving, a habit of persistent networking, or an ability to see underlying patterns in work processes.

Once the bones of the model had been assembled, we searched the writings of the most well-respected business minds in the country: Peter Drucker, Tom Peters, Jim Collins, Margaret Wheatley, Peter Senge, and others. More recently, we looked at the research conducted by psychologists and writers who were especially interested in 'chance' and how to prepare for it and to capitalize on it. We wanted to validate the model we were building. What emerged is a set of skills combining interpersonal facility and system understanding - a kind of blueprint for significant organizational contribution, a roadmap to becoming a key contributor and an indispensable asset to any organization.

It is important to point out that this model is not a *'theory'*. It is not simply the musings of experienced consultants. This model is built around real-life data that illustrate what it takes to be indispensable - to survive and to thrive in the new organization. The model has been tested in the crucible of real-life organization performance. Most important of all, this is data generated by those in a unique position to know:

- Those individual contributors who had been identified as

indispensable, and

- Those managers and supervisors who have gone through the process of choosing the best and brightest among *all* the qualified candidates to staff their organizations.

As we have talked to people about the model and developed training programs using the model, we have been rewarded with comments like:

- 'I always knew this but never really verbalized it in that way or thought about it much. That's just the way I (and other successful people) do things'.
- 'That really fits with my experience because ...'

How This Book Will Help You Become Indispensable

Why do some survive and thrive while other equally talented individuals fail to live up to the challenges during tough economic times and periods of organizational churn? Why are some individuals seen as indispensable while others simply represent a salary to be saved when the organization tightens its belt? How do some individuals contribute to an organization's mission and vision and propel their companies to high levels of performance while others get lost in day-to-day, non-remarkable drudgery?

This book answers those questions. It captures true information about those who become organization drivers and who are viewed as indispensable to their companies. Those who *'get it'* - who understand the implications of developing a set of 'essential skills' - will be those who survive and thrive, and become indispensable in their organizations, leading their companies to greatness. Those who don't will be left behind to complain about the demise of the 'good old days' when companies 'took care of their employees'.

You may be wondering at this point if it's possible to change your approach if you decide you want to embark on this journey. The answer is 'probably not' at a fundamental level. In terms of your basic personality style, it's not easy to change who you are at the deepest levels where spontaneous thoughts, actions, and beliefs originate. Nor should you want to. That's not what is required here.

31

Rather, it is highly possible to make changes in your attitudes and behaviors and to develop new coping abilities.

This book highlights research findings that connect with and reinforce the 'essential talents' and 'qualities of indispensability' that we discovered through our surveys. But it's not only *what* you know that makes a difference in making a contribution, it's how you *apply* that knowledge. That's why each chapter includes a catalog of applications, exercises, and suggested ways to put each of the skills into practice in your work. Finally, the book provides self-assessment surveys for each skill to help you identify and build on your strengths. In addition, you will get worksheets and planning guides to help you to map out a strategy to become indispensable in your organization.

How This Book Is Different

Over the years, there have been a few attempts at chronicling 'success skills for the 21st century'. Often the same traits are listed:

- Imagination
- Stamina
- Desire for results
- Good communication skills
- Team skills

For the most part, however, these lists of habits or skills lack any coherent framework for fully understanding these 'essential' skills and what has caused them to evolve. This book provides the model that ties these skills together in a way that makes them useful and practical.

Be clear. This book is about learning. But it's not about the kind of 'learning' that companies are so fond of spending millions for each year. *That* kind of learning can generally be boiled down into one of three categories.

1. **Useful but boring:** Sure, networking your PC to the office mega-system so that you have access to daily

updates on the newest productivity-enhancing software sure looks good come performance-review time. But let's face it - when you have a computer question, you're just going to call the IT geeks anyway.

2. **Buzzword city:** Everybody gathers in the company auditorium and listens to a sage on a stage toss around words like 'paradigm shift', 'creative collaboration', and 'learning organization'. Then we all return to our cubicles and do what we're told to do by someone with more organizational clout.

3. **Useless but fun:** A couple of days of trust falls, ziplining, and seeing your colleagues in their shorts in some tropical locale is fun. But afterwards everyone returns to the office, all bubbly and motivated, until they realize - usually within the first week back or when the first crisis hits, whichever comes first - that nothing or no one at work has *really* changed and the same old problems persist.

There is a fourth category - a form of learning that is useful, interesting, and relevant to your success. And the good news is that you don't even have to leave your office to partake. In fact, this kind of learning is best done *in vivo* - that's with you in place, trying things out, learning and making connections yourself, and seeing the results. Let's call this type of learning:

4. **'Kinetic learning':** to highlight its action-oriented nature.

Pure knowledge - the kind you get from books and lectures only gives you the *possibility* of action. It's potential energy. It's incomplete until it's put to good use. *Applied* knowledge is the key to organizational contribution. It's *kinetic energy*. It turns knowledge into action. It often makes the difference between being the one who is considered indispensable and the one who is overlooked - the difference between winning and losing.

The most meaningful type of experience, of course, is real-life experience: experience forged in our own organizational context. In this book, I will ask you to engage in a form of learning by doing.

We'll call this 'deliberate practice'. It means practicing with specific objectives in mind: in this case, the objective of becoming indispensable to your company and helping the organization survive and achieve high performance in the bargain.

So let's get started on the journey. But first, let's have a look at how habits are formed.

A Word About Habits

In research published in the *European Journal of Social Psychology,* Phillippa Lally and her colleagues at the *University College London* investigated the process of habit formation in everyday life. Ninety-six volunteers chose an eating, drinking or other kind of activity to carry out daily in the same context - for example 'after breakfast' - for 12 weeks. The time it took participants to reach '*automaticity*' (when a behavior becomes automatic enough that you perform it without thinking about it) ranged from 18 to 254 days. These findings show there is a wide variation in how long it could take you to form a habit.

In another series of studies, Dr. Elliot Berkman, Director of the *Social and Affective Neuroscience Lab* in the Department of Psychology *at the University of Oregon* showed that there are three main factors that can impact the amount of time it takes to change a habit.

First, breaking a habit really involves forming a new habit, or creating a new response to a trigger. The key here is to have an alternative habit available so you can engage in some type of *activity* instead of just focusing on resisting your former behavior. For example, people who are trying to quit smoking are more successful if they use aids such as gum or some type of replacement behavior rather than using a more passive approach such as a nicotine patch.

Second, the amount of motivation you have to change makes a difference. Those who want to form a new habit in order to live more in line with their own personal values are more likely to adjust their behaviors faster than those whose motivation is coming from external forces, such as societal or familial pressure.

Third, one's mental and physical ability to form a new habit comes into play. Habits that have been a part of one's life forever are ingrained at a neural level, making them strong determinants of behavior. For example, if you have had a soda for dinner every night since you were a child, replacing that with a healthier option is going to be quite a challenge. But, if you've never tried meditation before and you want to start practicing for a few minutes every night before bed, that would be an easier change to make.

So, as you navigate the *Phoenix Factor Model*, with the idea of capitalizing on your current strengths and putting in place new habits, consider how you might best facilitate your personal *habit development* and begin a new journey.

Chapter One

Two Prevailing Orientations That Make You Indispensable

What Our Surveys Showed

At the core of our model are two key capabilities: *Initiative* and *Collaboration*. These inherent orientations pull you up and forward. They are thought to be fundamental value choices, present in all of us. Humans have a natural tendency - as voluminous research on the topic has taught us - to act decisively, to seek achievement [6] (*Personal Initiative*), and to associate with and cooperate with others for the common good [7] (*Collaboration*). At one level, we are concerned about doing what needs to be done for own self-interest. At the same time, we are social creatures - forming associations and friendships to meet a human need for connection. This desire for companionship and approval goes beyond just huddling together for survival as our prehistoric ancestors did. In fact, we struggle to reconcile these seemingly opposing parts of our nature - the desire for individual success and achievement, and the desire for connectedness. It's not that we are both social and striving by accident, we are both social and striving by nature - as a consequence of behavioral predispositions selected for over eons of evolutionary history.

These two orientations - *Initiative* and *Collaboration* - represent an 'Active' stance and a 'Receptive' nature in our make-up. They provide the initial guidance in our model. They are the 'uplifting' wings that, combined with the other skillsets, allow us to soar. Personal initiative is the booster rocket of organization effectiveness. It delivers the power and drive to be successful and, ultimately to become indispensable. Collaboration is the social glue that holds together many of the essential skills we will detail in later chapters. As we began to build our model, we started with these two core competencies.

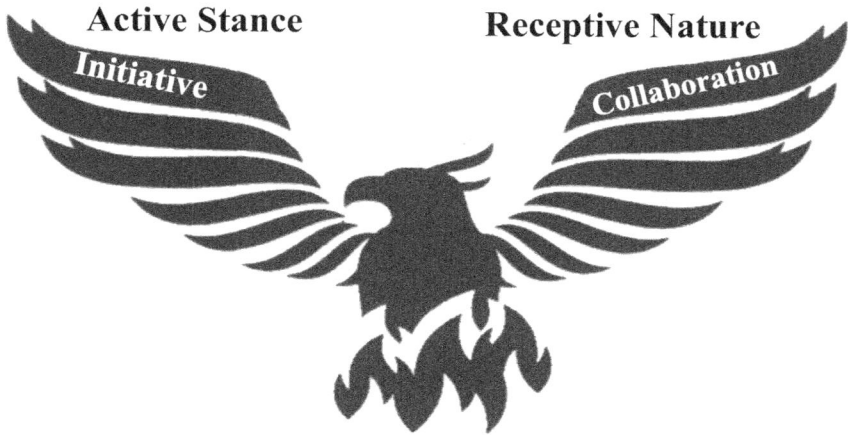

Active Stance   **Receptive Nature**

Initiative   Collaboration

Measure Your Prevailing Orientation

In the following brief assessment, you will identify the strength of two prevailing orientations in your approach to the world - those elements that initially pull you up and forward. This self-assessment will set the stage for assisting you in building your capacity for indispensable organizational contribution.

For each of the following 30 pairs of value descriptors, you are to circle, from each pair, the one *most* descriptive of you. You may feel that both qualities describe you - or that neither does. But for each pair, you *must* choose *one*. You are to select the option that best describes you. Sometimes it may be difficult to select between the two statements because you feel they both are descriptive of you, or that neither is. Don't worry, that's the way it is supposed to be. We have deliberately paired statements that are not polar opposites. As you make your selections, you are creating a pattern of choices. You are describing what you feel is 'most characteristic' of you in a 'forced choice' manner. It is the pattern of choices that will be the most revealing, rather than any specific choice. There is no right or best choice to any pairing. As you go through the instrument, try not to overanalyze the choices or second-guess how you think you should respond. Simply pick the option that feels best to you. Total the number of choices you circled at the bottom of each column.

<u>A</u>	<u>B</u>
Decisive	Collaborative
Self-Confident	Accepting
Ambitious	Trusting
Competitive	Charming
Optimistic	Sociable
Persistent	Helpful
Knowledgeable	Interested
Competent	Attentive
Industrious	Cooperative
Proactive	Considerate
Results-Oriented	Responsive
Action-Oriented	Team Player
Self-Reliant	Uniting
Initiating	Outgoing
Self-Motivated	Gregarious
Risk-Taker	Approachable
Problem Solver	Involved
Responsible	Encouraging
Achievement-Oriented	Participating
Enterprising	Accommodating
Assertive	Noncompetitive
Self-Directed	Open-Minded
Self-Assured	Receptive
Resourceful	Adaptable
Determined	Interactive
Eager	Understanding
Pioneering	Communicator
Positive	Supportive
Individualistic	Tactful
Driven	Influential
TOTALS:_____	_____
Initiative	*Collaboration*

What You Know… Instinctively

We all know that we have the ability to make the work of our colleagues easier or more difficult, if we've a mind to. The decision we make is largely determined by our willingness to take personal initiative to solve work problems, and by our willingness to consider others and involve them when appropriate.

Our survey results indicate that 87% of our respondents identified some form of either initiative or collaboration as a key capability for success inside the 21st century organization. And, although both orientations were seen as of high value, the most sought-after individual of all was the one who had *both* these inclinations in balance.

On this short self-rating quiz, if your endorsements indicate a marked preference for one column's descriptors over the other, your prevailing orientations are out of balance - one wing is stronger than the other. If your total score in the *Initiative* column is much greater than your total score in the *Collaboration* column, for example, you may be systematically avoiding the expression of collaboration or systematically choosing personal initiative as your primary work style. While it is true that all of us have the capacity for both orientations, we often emphasize one over the other when we work. The assessment instrument's 'forced choice' format allows you to determine your typical, most preferred stance.

Look at those items that you *did not circle* in the column where you scored the lowest. To bring your prevailing orientations back into balance, begin to think of ways in which you can incorporate those (non-endorsed) value choices into your work style. Remember, organizations appreciate both *Initiative* **and** the capacity for *Collaboration*. But the most valued organization member of all is the individual who has *both of these key capabilities in balance*.

Turn to Table 1 in the Appendix: *Your Key Contributor Profile.* Enter your scores on the two prevailing orientations: *Initiative* and *Collaboration*. You will use these scores later to begin to build your *Key Contributor Ready Kit*. If you would like to increase the expression of either initiative or collaboration in your work style, the tips that appear later in this chapter will help you to sharpen those orientations. Initiative Skill Builders and Collaboration Skill Builders are detailed in the chapter sections following the explanation of each of the orientations.

Personal Initiative

"The secret of getting ahead is getting started."

\- Agatha Christie

Personal Initiative: A Rare and Powerful Commodity

In my consulting work I often have the task of assisting organizations in looking at how their employees manage the unpredictable - the crises that organizations face. My estimate of typical employee capabilities, drawn from my work in dozens of organizations, is as follows:

- Percentage of employees who ignore or misjudge the early warning signs of a crisis - about 60%
- Percentage of employees who do some investigating about the nature of the crisis - about 30%
- Percentage of employees who evaluate the crisis properly and take appropriate action - about 10%

The Organization Driver

Key contributors know that great opportunities are always present, no matter what the condition of the organization. A weakness in the organization can be an avenue to show your skill and leadership. Instead of waiting for 'them' to take care of it, contributors get busy, show initiative, and take a risk. Contributors attach their sense of self-worth to tangible results - setting clear goals and pushing to achieve them. For contributors it is the active deed - *accomplishment* - that is satisfying. Outward, energetic action defines their personal style.

In our model, *Personal Initiative* includes four more specific aptitudes:
1. Proactivity
2. An Internal Locus of Control
3. An Achievement Orientation
4. Hope and Confidence

Let's have a closer look at each of these specific aptitudes.

1. Proactivity

"When a great moment knocks on the door of your life, it is often no louder than the beating of your heart, and it is very easy to miss it."

- Boris Pasternak

Fortune Favors the Bold [8]

A graduating class from *Princeton University* was celebrating their 25th anniversary. They decided to survey their classmates in a number of areas. One question on the survey asked the graduates to think back 25 years, comparing how they were doing currently to the aspirations they held on graduation day 25 years earlier. About 40% of the graduates stated that they were 'pleasantly surprised and happy' about how their lives had turned out. Another 40% rated themselves as 'content but not surprised' with their station in life. The final 20% stated that they were 'disappointed' in how their lives had turned out compared to what they had hoped for themselves on graduation day. No big surprises here. Some of us achieve our goals and more, while others of us lag behind what we judge to be our potential.

The more interesting finding came from the graduates' responses to a second question on the survey. The question asked, 'How many different jobs have you held since graduation'? or 'How many different ventures have you launched'? The top 40% of the graduates - the ones who had rated themselves as 'pleasantly surprised and happy' with their lot in life - had held six or more jobs or launched six or more ventures in those 25 years - far more than their colleagues who had rated themselves as either 'content but not surprised' or 'disappointed' in how their lives had turned out.[9]

Key contributors know that to be effective, one must act. Success depends on what you do, not just on your reflections or speculations. In their organizations, contributors see what needs to be done and find ways to do it. They show a willingness to take the lead, to take the action necessary to move forward, rather than wait and react to circumstances as they unfold. For key contributors, their motivation appears largely from within and seems to stem from some deeply felt personal goals. They believe that success comes due to dogged determination and follow-through.

The following quotes about significant contributors are typical and are drawn directly from our surveys:

> "We had several projects that had been talked over for months. When he got the assignments, things started happening".

> "She was a doer rather than a delegator. If something looked like it might get dicey, she would take responsibility herself".

> "If he has an idea, he has a plan to make it happen".

> "She wasn't inclined to sit around and think about things for too long. Her style was to take action, and she almost always knew what to do".

> "He notices what needs attention and what needs to be done, and others follow his lead".

> "He is considered to be the 'take-charge' person in our organization and steps up to the plate when no one else is willing to".

2. An Internal Locus of Control

"Wisdom is knowing what path to take next. Integrity is taking it".
- Robyn Elpruhzlein

> **Don't Just Stand There... Do Something!**
>
> A study at a major software development firm contrasted 'average performers' with 'top performers' in that high-tech organization.[10] Both groups said taking the initiative was important, but they differed in what they would do. Average performers said they would write a memo to their supervisor if they discovered a software bug. Top performers would fix the bug.
>
> The managers in that organization reported that for their top performers, doing the job meant figuring out how to solve many problems themselves. If their solutions worked most of the time, they got promoted.

An *internal locus of control* is just a fancy way of saying that key contributors believe their fate is in their own hands. They are comfortable with independent action and develop a knack for overcoming or outsmarting any roadblocks that might get in the way.

The following quotes about key organization contributors are typical and are drawn directly from our surveys:

> "He could kick down any door that stood in the way. If there was an obstacle to be overcome, we gave him the assignment".

> "Her motivation is internal. She doesn't need any pep talks".

> "He is quite independent, accustomed to going his own way - making decisions and taking action on his own. And he's usually right".

> "He is extremely impatient with delay, indecision, and excessive reflection. But he gets things done".

> "She is self-reliant and independent and has the capacity for independent thinking and action".

43

"He gets things done when he says he will. He doesn't make commitments that he can't keep. This is a guy we can count on".

3. An Achievement Orientation

"Well done is better than well said".

- Benjamin Franklin

I Can't Help It. For Some Reason, I Just Perform Better.

A recent study bearing on achievement motivation produced some fascinating results.[11] In the first of two parts of the experiment, psychologists had participants complete a word search task. One half of the participants' puzzles included words associated with achievement (e.g., "strive," "succeed," "first," and "win"), while the other half performed a motivationally neutral puzzle including words such as: "carpet," "diamond," and "hat." This part of the experiment was designed to create, in the first group, a motive to achieve - even though participants were unaware of the presence of these *'seed'* words. The second group of participants had no such created 'unconscious' need to achieve.

Following this initial step, participants then performed a computerized simulation of running a factory. Their goal in the simulation was to produce a specific number of 'widgets'. They were only told, however, that they could change the number of employees in the factory. Although participants were not told about the complex causal relationship that existed between the number of employees and past 'widget' production levels (and they could not verbalize the relationship after the experiment had ended), over several trials they all gradually grew better in controlling the factory and in increasing production. But the 'unconsciously motivated' participants (the group that had previously found words associated with achievement) learned to control the factory far better than the control group. The results indicate that those who have an achievement orientation - even when this orientation has been created below their conscious awareness - perform at higher, more effective levels.

Key contributors are self-directed learners and problem solvers. Opportunities for advancement and personal challenge are important to them. They actively seek stretch assignments and opportunities that put them to the test. They continually seek to expand their abilities and sharpen their skills. Self-assurance and self-confidence are also part of this mix. Leading by example through an orientation that stresses achievement is the operating style of the initiating contributor.

The following quotes about key contributors are typical and are drawn directly from our surveys:

> "He likes to be the one making the decisions and steering the course of what's happening, and he's usually the best one for the job".

> "She always seemed to have a goal in mind and was working toward something".

> "This guy sticks his neck out on the high-profile assignments, and he almost always comes through for us".

> "She is not shy about expecting recognition equal to her contributions, and she deserves it".

> "He seems to be continually seeking new challenges and new experiences".

> "He is someone who can be counted on to move in and seize an opportunity or create one".

4. Hope and Confidence

"We judge ourselves by what we feel capable of doing, while others judge us by what we have already done."
- Henry Wadsworth Longfellow

45

Hope: The Stuff of Success

Martin Seligman, director of the *Positive Psychology Center* at the *University of Pennsylvania*, has devoted much of his career to the study of human helplessness and its antithesis - optimism. In his book *Learned Optimism* [12], Seligman focused on what he terms "explanatory style", that is, the thoughts we use to explain and understand the events that happen to us in our personal and work lives. Seligman believes that the key to understanding why different people respond differently to similar events is attributable to the differences in how each person privately interprets or explains the event. Seligman identified three elements of explanatory style:

- **Permanence**: The extent to which I view the situation I am facing as unlikely to ever change, rather than as a temporary glitch: *"Things never work out in my favor"* vs. *"I'm having a bad day today"*.
- **Personalization:** The extent to which I believe the outcome I am experiencing is a result of my own doing, or whether I believe it is the result of luck, chance, or the actions of others: *"I can be successful by applying effort and working hard"* vs. *"I was lucky to get an easy assignment this time"*. The savvy reader will note that this quality bears a striking relationship to an *internal locus of control*.
- **Pervasiveness**: The extent to which I believe the outcome of one specific event will color my entire experience of life, or whether I believe that this outcome is confined to just this one specific area: *"I'm not a very smart person"* vs. *"I'm bad at mental math problems"*.

Although how we explain our successes is important, Seligman discovered that how we explain our *'failures'* and setbacks is even more important. In a series of research studies, Seligman showed that whether or not we have *'hope'* depends on two dimensions of our explanatory style: pervasiveness and permanence. Finding specific and temporary causes for misfortune is the art of hope. Specific causes limit helplessness only to the original situation, and temporary causes limit helplessness in time. On the other hand, universal causes spread helplessness through all our endeavors, and permanent causes produce helplessness far into the future. Finding universal and permanent causes for misfortune is the practice of despair.

The optimistic style of explaining good events is the opposite of that used for bad events: it's internal rather than external. People who believe they cause good things tend to like themselves better than people who believe good things come from other people, from circumstances, or from luck. To quote Seligman: "Success requires persistence, the ability to not give up in the face of failure. I believe that an optimistic explanatory style is the key to persistence".

This quality of hope and confidence is much different than just rosy cheerfulness. Rather, it is the expectation that you can prevail over obstacles through your own efforts. Key contributors stand out from the crowd because of their enduring hope for the future and the belief that with the right combination of effort and perseverance, success is just around the corner. They tend to focus on what *can* happen, rather than on what the obstacles are. When there is light at the end of the tunnel, they don't build more tunnel. The organization contributors we found displayed the 'hope' that allowed them to be persistent and successful in their efforts.

The following quotes about key contributors are typical and are drawn directly from our surveys:

> "When something isn't going right, he is the one who wants to find out why and fix it".

> "She will stay with a difficult or challenging situation to prove it can be done".

> "He believes that if you want things to happen, you've got to make them happen and convince people to trust in your competence. You can't wait for things to come to you".

> "She can make all kinds of decisions with a minimum of fuss and panic".

"He is exceedingly self-assured and self-confident - which leads to his performing well in most situations".

Stock Your Key Contributor Ready Kit

In the section that follows (and in the final sections of each of Chapters Two through Five), we will detail tips ('Skill Builders') for how to increase your ability to be a key organization contributor and how to stock your kit with the skills you need to be indispensable in your organization. We designate some tips with an ☼ icon, indicating a tip that is likely to result in you being seen as indispensable (a star) in your organization. Other tips will be designated with a Δ icon - the delta symbol indicating change. These activities will result in you being seen as someone who works for the good of the enterprise. But the higher-ups will recognize that you're a valuable asset to have around because your actions also change the organization for the better. A final set of tips are designed with a ♘ icon (a horseshoe). These tips refer to a *'luck adjustment'* – positioning yourself to take advantage of good luck that may come your way or mitigating any effects of bad luck that may be visited upon you.

Build Your Personal Initiative: Become an Organization Driver

Our surveys with high-impact organizational contributors, and the managers who hire them, make it clear that one key to being indispensable in your company is cultivating the orientation of personal initiative. This represents a willingness to take the lead in solving work problems, the inclination to take the action necessary to move forward - to act, doing what needs to be done for the good of the enterprise - rather than waiting and reacting to circumstances as they unfold. Key contributors know that to be effective, one must act. Success depends on what you do, not just on your reflections or speculations. Contributors see what needs to be done and find ways to do it. This orientation comes more naturally to some, but it is a skill that is learnable for everyone.

If you want to add to your capability in the area of personal initiative, here are some how-to's to help you sharpen this capacity.

As you read through the Skill Builders associated with each aspect of personal initiative, circle the symbol beside those you would like to implement as part of your *Key Contributor Ready Kit*. Then use Table 2 in the Appendix to fill out aspects of your *'Initiative Kit'*.

1. Proactivity

Key contributors understand that great opportunities are always present. Instead of waiting, they get busy, spring into action, and take a risk. Their self-worth seems attached to the tangible results they can create. For key contributors it is the active deed - accomplishment - that is satisfying. Outward, energetic action defines their personal style.

Skill Builders:

U Get in the game. Researchers who study the characteristics of 'lucky' (as opposed to 'unlucky') people have identified a trait they refer to as *'constructive supernaturalism'*[13]. They point out that dealing with unseen powers is essentially the definition of luck. A reliance on something supernatural – a 'lucky' talisman, 'lucky' numbers, a horoscope, or even something more orthodox such as 'divine intervention' helps people get lucky because it allows them to make otherwise impossible choices. It helps by allowing you to get into a potentially winning position. To put it in common sense terms: Before that lottery ticket won the jackpot, someone had to buy it.

Δ Be a detective in your organization. Look for what needs to be done.
- What trends do you see?
- What opportunities are on the horizon in your industry?

- What do you hear from your customers that, if put into practice, would improve your organization's response?
- What is the organization *not* doing that would be more effective?
- Who could you talk to about this ... or better yet, what can *you* do?

Once you've got a hot spot in mind, swing into action. Take some first steps. Take a look at the results you are getting and retool, if necessary. Once you have a bead on what needs to be done, and how, schedule a sit-down with the person who can officially authorize your plan. Even if you don't get approval immediately, your initiative will be recognized by those who count, and you'll be on their radar screen as someone to look to for ideas to improve the company!

☼   Try to discover at least one untapped opportunity within your area of responsibility each day and make a step (even a small one) toward capitalizing on that opportunity. Ask yourself, 'What part of this looks interesting to me'? Then do it! An added benefit of this approach? When you work on interesting tasks, your workday is much more personally fulfilling. Time spent designing a new product or solving a persistent organizational problem is a lot more fulfilling than filling out the weekly production report.

☼   Got a free minute? Tell whoever you report to that you've finished your project earlier than expected and that you're available. If you want the plum assignments, don't be afraid to say you have the time to take it on. Demonstrate that you can not only do your job, but somebody else's as well. Roll up your sleeves and volunteer for assignments that might be interesting.

☼   Fill empty spaces. When you see an opportunity to work on a new project, jump on it. You never know what opportunities lay just around the corner... and you'll develop a reputation as a go-getter.

☼   Embrace the mind-set of *'Ready – Fire – Aim'*. This is a concept that was first conceived by Tom Peters and Bob Waterman, in their landmark book *In Search of Excellence*.[14] The essence of the approach is this: get your product or idea out there as quickly as possible. You can refine and polish more carefully after you're in the game. Contributors prefer to put *some* plan into action, maybe at the expense of a *perfect* first response, but with the advantage of getting quick feedback and making the necessary adjustments. Your goal is to establish your presence in the marketplace of products or ideas. Here's the strategy:

- *Ready:* Set your general direction. Get a vision of where you're going and what you want to accomplish. It may not be much more than a compass heading at this point. Remember, key contributors are those who can adapt, flex, and even change direction if need be.
- *Fire:* Get started. Do something. Get some movement going to overcome the inertia. Remember the probability game: the more things you do, the greater are your chances of being ultimately successful. Contributors experiment. Don't be afraid to get moving, even if you're not sure it's the 100% right thing to do.
- *Aim:* Now that you are moving, clipping along, firing on all cylinders, it's time to "sight in" your target. Fine-tune, adjust, adapt. By this time you're in the marketplace… you're ahead of the game, and your initiative will not go unnoticed by those who count.

The Perils of Procrastination and How to Defeat the Impulse

A recent study by an international team of psychologists focused on whether there might be a link between how we think about a task and our tendency to postpone it.[15] In other words, are we more likely to see some tasks as 'psychologically distant' - thus making us save them for later rather than tackling them right now? The psychologists gave questionnaires to groups of students and asked them to respond by email. All the questions had to do with some

---

mundane task, such as opening a bank account. But different groups of students were given different instructions for answering the questions. Some were to write about what the activity implied about personal traits - what kind of person has a bank account, for example. The other group wrote simply about the steps in the process - speaking to a bank officer, filling out forms, making an initial deposit, and so forth. There proved to be a significant difference between the response times of the two groups. Even though all of the students were being paid for completion of the task, those who thought about the questions in more abstract terms were more likely to procrastinate. In fact, some never completed the task at all. By contrast, those who were focused on the how, when, and where of the task hopped right on the assignment and completed it rather than delaying it. The psychologists concluded that merely thinking about the task in more concrete, specific terms makes it feel like it should be completed sooner and reduced procrastination.

Skill Builders:

☼ Always try to do 10% of each task assigned to you immediately. This way you can better see what it's going to take to finish the rest. Ask yourself: 'Based on what I have done, what else can I do to move this project along'? Take some action each day on the assignments you have been given.

2. Internal Locus of Control

This is a fancy way of saying that key contributors believe their fate is in their own hands. They are comfortable with independent action and develop a knack for overcoming or outsmarting any roadblock. They're '*hurdlers*'.

Skill Builders:

☼ Be '*response-able*'. Ask yourself, 'What response *can* I make in this situation'? Avoid the thought: 'There's nothing I can do about that…' Preface your thoughts about some project or obstacle with the prompt 'How can I _____'?

'How-to' language and thought leads to possibilities, to options, to alternatives, to choices … to success.

☼ What actions, possibilities, alternatives fall within your circle of influence? Don't invest in thinking, worrying, or obsessing about those things over which you have absolutely no control or influence. Rather, devote your energies only to those things that you can affect directly or influence indirectly. When you put your energy into those things that you *can* control, your influence (and your results) begin to grow like magic… and your circle of influence begins to expand.

Δ When you get a great idea, think through the basics of a plan to make it happen. If you spot an obstacle, think of a way around it. Even if you only have the first few steps, you'll begin to develop a reputation as someone who can see past problems to organizational opportunities.

☼ Seek out areas where a success would be a blockbuster for you. Try to identify the high-payoff, high-impact alternatives and devote your thinking to these. Ask yourself, 'What skills do I have that would work here'? Build an action plan that includes these activities and the steps you could take to pursue these opportunities (regardless of whether they are currently within your area of responsibility). Then, discuss these ideas with those who have the power to grant you the freedom to pursue these activities. Higher-ups love 'a man with a plan'. You'll develop a reputation as someone who can see past the problems and find organizational opportunities.

3. An Achievement Orientation [16]

Key contributors are self-directed learners and problem solvers. Opportunities for advancement and personal challenge are important to them. They actively seek opportunities that test their abilities.

53

Skill Builders:

☼   Always have a set of personal and career goals you are working toward. It makes it easier to guide your initiatives. Where do you want to be in your career one year from now? five years from now? ten years from now? What events, activities, people, or places will move you in the direction you want to go?

☼   Ask for feedback and use it to improve your performance. Get a good 360 evaluation. Ask for feedback from your colleagues. What could you do to help *them* be more successful? Ask your boss. What more could you be doing to contribute to the enterprise? Even if they can't come up with anything specific the first time you ask, you'll be pegged as an up-and-comer... someone who has the good of the company at heart.

☼   Follow through religiously on your commitments. This is what distinguishes a key contributor from a *'fly-by-nighter'*. In addition, when you follow through on all your commitments, suddenly you are among the 10% who do. You'll become known as someone who can be counted on, someone people want on their team, someone who is, well... indispensable!

4. A Sense of Hope and Confidence

This is *not* looking at the world through rose-colored glasses. Rather, it is the contributor's expectation that he or she can prevail over any obstacle through his or her own efforts. They show an enduring hope for the future and a belief that with the right combination of effort and perseverance, success is just around the corner. Quite frankly, hang around with a key contributor for a while, and this outlook becomes downright contagious.

The Biochemistry of Hope

Dr. Jerome Groopman has studied how the brain interacts with the experience of hope.[17] His findings? Your brain pumps chemicals responsible for the hopeful sensation, which in turn block out pain and accelerate healing. Belief and positive expectation - the one-two punch of hope - release neurochemicals, endorphins, and enkephalins that mimic the effects of morphine. As a result, hope helps us overcome hurdles we could not otherwise scale.

Skill Builders:

U   Want to boost your confidence? Make a 'success list' of those things that have gone extraordinarily well due to your efforts. Sit with it for a while. Things may not bubble up immediately (especially if things have been rough around work recently). But, eventually, recollections of your spectacular accomplishments will surface. Now, capture the learning.

- What did you do to make this happen?
- What skills did you use?
- How did you proceed?
- Whose help did you solicit?

Don't lose this information. It will prove valuable as you create additional successes and will do wonders for your outlook and your confidence in your abilities.

Collaboration

"We're all angels with only one wing. We can only fly while embracing each other".

> -   Luciano de Crescenzo,
> twentieth-century Italian poet

The 21st century will be unfriendly to those superhero types who try to wing heavenward by sheer force of will, ignoring all those around them. Success will belong to those whose knowledge and effort are widely shared with colleagues. Collaboration with those who depend on you for their work, and on whom you depend for information and product to get your own work out, makes perfect sense.

Involve Others and Multiply Your Impact

Key contributors choose to be *ambassadors* - people who help their colleagues understand, who explain the benefits of a course of action, and who work to move others forward along with them. Those who are less effective in their work hoard information, become locked in fierce competitive struggles with their own colleagues, and try to go it on their own. Contributors establish themselves not as power brokers, but as people of influence - able to work effectively with a variety of individuals, including those over whom they have little direct authority or control.

The capacity for collaboration describes a strong desire to include others, when appropriate, to leverage impact and involvement. This is the desire to work for the common good, accessing all the human resources in the organization. There is an element of social awareness and a sensitivity to the needs of others. There is the belief that people are important and that working and making decisions with other people is a preference. It's a mind-set of cooperation and interdependence. Involving others by using persuasive methods and eliciting cooperation by explaining the rationale for any proposed action is the contributor's talent. Knowing lots of people and getting along well with others is the key. Key contributors have an ability to gain the respect and confidence of various types of people and, in interacting with others, they manifest a generally amiable and easygoing manner.

It's easy to make a case that *Personal Initiative* comes naturally and is an important skill. It virtually calls out: 'survival of the fittest'. Somewhat more difficult is to make the same case for *Collaboration*. Many of us have been led to believe that the real success stories involve individuals who go it alone, who rely on their own wits and skills to pull off a win. At times, in an achievement-oriented culture, there is the sense that asking for help from others is a sign of weakness. But there is ample research evidence to suggest that collaboration does serve a survival function. You may remember from the stories of the Plymouth Pilgrims, Ben Franklin, Lewis and Clark and Dale Carnegie that they all recognized the value of collaboration.

It's In Our Genes

Research that has focused on the social sentiments such as sympathy, empathy, fairness, and sociability has revealed that these traits are naturally occurring - they're programmed into our way of being as humans.[18] We know this because their absence is noted as aberrant or unusual. For example, those without empathy are labeled sociopaths.

These studies show that newborns engage in rudimentary social behavior before they are taught. They express distress at the sound of other babies crying. They prefer human sounds to any other sound. Even babies born blind will smile. Babies born both deaf and blind will laugh during play.

In addition, there is a rudimentary moral judgment (*'fairness'*) made at a very early age. Even as children begin to speak, before they have had the chance to be taught a complex social skill like sharing, they indicate a knowledge that such sharing is something that they ought to do.

Within two years of age, pro-social behaviors are obvious. Very young children show off things and ask for a response – 'Look at this….' They share, they help, they bring things for us to see, and they console those who seem upset.

Individuals who have just given blood feel gratified. The crowd cheers when *our team* is victorious even though we know no one on the team. Sociobiologists tell us that individuals with pro-social impulses had greater reproductive success and therefore greater 'survival value'. We have been 'prepared' biologically for collaborating with others.[19]

Indeed, those who become key contributors have moved away from thinking 'competitive advantage', especially as it applies to their own colleagues. Instead, they seek a *'collaborative advantage'*.

The capacity for collaboration has to do with what has been termed 'social capital' - the ability for people to work together for common purposes. The concept of human capital starts from the premise that in 21st century organizations, capital is embodied less in land, factories, tools, and machines, and increasingly lies in the knowledge that resides inside the human mind. Social capital has to do with people's ability to associate with, and work effectively with, one another. Now the critical differences between companies truly lie in the utilization of their human resources. It's not just lip service any longer. In the companies I have consulted with over the years, it has been abundantly clear that it is the *quality* of the interpersonal environment - *how* and *how well* the employees worked together - that determined a company's success or failure. This capacity is critical to economic life as well as virtually every other aspect of human existence.

In our model, *Collaboration* involves three more specific aptitudes:

1. An Orientation Toward Others
2. Responsiveness to the Needs of Others: Listening, Helping, and Cooperating
3. Polished People Skills

1. An Orientation Toward Others

"Talent wins games, but teamwork wins championships".
- Michael Jordan

All for One and One for All

In the army when a platoon goes out for a five-mile run, everyone starts out together. But if a group starts to straggle, the whole platoon will run back around the stragglers and recreate the group. After a while, another group begins to straggle, and the platoon circles back again. The platoon learns to move forward in a series of recurring circles that helps everyone get to the final destination.

The people who really see the future pull others along with them. But if they get too far out in front and don't circle back, they lose their colleagues. The corporate equivalent of circling back is the use of all the *i*-words: *'information', 'involvement', 'inclusion'.*

Our interviews and surveys made it clear that key contributors take the social initiative *and* show a participative temperament. They involve others. They much prefer to work and make decisions with other people rather than toiling alone.

The following quotes about contributors are typical and are drawn directly from our surveys:

> "He communicates an attitude that people are important".

> "He preferred to work with and make decisions with other people, as opposed to going it alone, and he has been remarkably successful in this way".

> "He believes that it is always necessary for people to cooperate with one another for things to run smoothly. He has been willing to include even people whom others have found to be difficult to work with".

> "She can make participatory management work".

> "He is very gregarious and can really elicit the group's support when it is needed".

> "She is socially aware and very sensitive to the subtleties of interpersonal relationships. This is an attitude that has served her well in our organization".

2. Responsiveness to the Needs of Others: Listening, Helping, and Cooperating

"Innovation, everyday entrepreneurship, and creativity are the results of collaboration".

- Peter Keen

The Prisoner's Dilemma [20]

Consider a widely-researched two-person game. The game was first framed as a game in which two suspects are arrested by the police.

The police have insufficient evidence for a conviction and, having separated both prisoners, visit each of them to offer each the same deal. If one testifies for the prosecution against the other (defects) and the other remains silent (cooperates), the betrayer goes free and the silent accomplice receives the full ten-year sentence. If both remain silent, both prisoners are sentenced to only six months in jail for a minor charge. If each betrays the other, each receives a five-year sentence. Each prisoner must choose to betray the other or to remain silent. Each one is assured that the other would not know about the betrayal before the end of the investigation. The game was originally framed to examine strategies of defection and cooperation.

The game has been morphed for study by psychologists and organizational theorists into a slightly different version. Each player is matched with another, and participants are given a few minutes to get to know their partner. Then they are separated into different rooms, and each is shown two buttons. You push one button to *cooperate* with the other player. You push the other button to *sabotage* him. If both players push cooperate, each wins two dollars. If both push sabotage, they win one dollar each. If one pushes cooperate and the other pushes sabotage, the saboteur wins three dollars and the cooperator gets nothing.

In repeated rounds, some players cooperate for a while and then try to trick their partner by sabotaging them and having a chance to greatly increase their personal payoff. Now and then, players get themselves locked into repeated, angry use of their sabotage button. (Who among us hasn't been led by anger into a lose-lose scenario?) But cooperation and maximization of mutual profit almost always eventually wins out and becomes the norm in iterated versions of the game.

Now for the most interesting part of the findings connected with this research. When players are subjected to MRI brain scans while they play, something strange occurs. Each cooperative win-win play releases dopamine - a neurotransmitter commonly associated with feelings of pleasure and enjoyment. In addition, such a cooperative play lights up the same pleasure centers in the brain as does, say, eating chocolate. [21]

Here's something key contributors understand: cooperation has a far more basic payoff than mere profit. Cooperation turns out to be an authentic physical pleasure.

Like good caregivers in every avenue of life, those with the capacity for collaboration are skilled at listening and offering feedback. They are able to anticipate others' needs and are ready to look after them. You'll set the table for yourself much more readily if you make an effort to make the work lives of others easier. When you cultivate a reputation as someone who rallies around others and helps, you make results happen in a much bigger way.

The following quotes about our contributors are typical and are drawn directly from our surveys:

> "Her personal responsiveness to the efforts of others is a real door-opener for her".

> "She helps others by being available and encouraging. She communicates, 'I'm here if you need me".

> "In conflict situations, he is one who really works to understand the other person's point of view".

> "He takes the social initiative and wants to create a participative climate".

> "He is patient with others, shows loyalty to the group, is a good listener, and shows sincere appreciation for the effort of others. He is truly able to create a motivational environment in his group".

> "She is genuinely interested in the welfare of the other people in the group and tries to establish a close relationship with all her coworkers".

> "One of his greatest strengths is his ability to clarify and build on the ideas of others".

4. **Polished People Skills**

> *"Anyone who doesn't get along with people doesn't belong in this business, because that's all we got around here".*
>
> - Lee Iacocca

Likability Counts

Tiziana Casciaro and Miguel Lobo, writing in *Harvard Business Review,* reported a study that focused on how we go about choosing those on the job with whom we want to be associated, and specifically with whom we would like to work.[22] In most cases, people choose their work partners according to two criteria: *competence* at the job (*Does Joe know what he's doing?*) and *likability (Is Mary enjoyable to work with?)* Obviously both things matter, but they interact in an interesting way. It is possible to categorize people at work along each of these two dimensions: more or less *competent* and more or less *likable*... and each style can be characterized in specific ways:

- Highly competent and highly likable: 'The Lovable Star'
- Highly competent but unlikable: 'The Competent Jerk'
- Low competence but highly likable: 'The Lovable Fool'
- Low competence and unlikable: 'The Incompetent Jerk'

Not surprisingly, social network surveys at four different organizations showed that everybody wanted to work with the 'Lovable Star' and nobody wanted to work with the 'Incompetent Jerk'. But things got a bit more interesting when people were faced with the choice between 'Competent Jerks' and 'Lovable Fools'. When mangers were asked about this choice, they most often said that when it comes to getting a job done, of course *competence* trumps *likability*. 'I can handle the guy being a jerk if he's competent, but I can't train someone who's incompetent'; or 'I really care about the knowledge and skills you bring to the table. If you're a nice person on top of that, that's just a bonus'. But despite what people might have *said* about their preferences, the reverse turned out to be true in practice. Likability played a much more important role in forming work relationships - not friendships at work - but job-oriented relationships. Likability served as a gathering factor. If someone is strongly disliked, it's almost irrelevant whether or not he is competent - people won't want to work with him anyway. By contrast, if someone is *liked*, his colleagues will seek out every little bit of competence he has to offer. Generally speaking, a little extra 'likability' goes a longer way than a little extra 'competence' in making you someone who is desirable to work with - and in increasing your chances to be seen as indispensable in your organization.

In a related study at *Bell Labs*, researchers from *Harvard University* studied e-mail patterns to determine why certain scientists underperformed their equally distinguished colleagues. What they found was that scientists who were *disliked* had been frozen out of the informal e-chat circles that distributed advice, gossip, and other useful information. When these pariahs asked for help from netmates in times of crisis, what they got was the cold e-shoulder.[23]

Another Reason to Bring on the Charm

Net Future Institute recently conducted a survey of 233 senior managers across several industries.[24] They found that 67% of these executives rely on 'likability' of a candidate when making hiring and promotion decisions. In fact, a candidate's actual 'job skills', at 62%, mattered slightly less than likability. Being likable isn't exactly everything, but the other key factors are pretty closely related. Some 73% of hiring managers said that they valued a candidate's 'likelihood to fit in' with the organization. The conclusion drawn by the research firm: building a sustainable career today increasingly requires a mix of technical ability and business savvy, as well as a heavy dose of likability as a personality factor.

There is just something about those who achieve the status of key organization contributor that exudes leadership, influence, and well – *charisma* - in everything they say and do. They have the ability to gain the trust, respect, and confidence of different types of people all over the organization. They have a warm and inviting presence that draws others to them.

The following quotes about our key contributors are typical and are drawn directly from our surveys:

> "Her leadership really comes from her ability to influence and motivate others".

> "He is liked by everyone because of his warmth, empathy, and understanding of others' situations, and he is able to work well with anyone".

> "He is seen as good-natured, easygoing, emotionally expressive, ready to cooperate, attentive to people, kindly, and adaptable".

> "He has a knack for surviving the wear and tear of dealing with people in grueling emotional situations without fatigue or anger".

> "He has the ability to create a favorable impression and to gain the respect and confidence of all kinds of different people in this huge organization".

> "He is extremely likable and can do and say the correct thing in social situations with a quality that other people admire".

Get the Right People on the Bus and Get On With Them

Our surveys with high-impact organizational contributors and the managers who hire them make it clear that one key to being indispensable in your company is cultivating the inclination for collaboration with others. This is shown through a desire to include others when appropriate to leverage impact and involvement… to work for the common good, accessing all the human resources in the organization. This orientation comes more naturally to some, but it is a skill that is learnable by everyone.

If you want to add to your capability in the area of *Collaboration*, here are some how-tos to help you sharpen this capacity.

As you read through the Skill Builders associated with each aspect of *Collaboration*, circle the symbol beside those you would like to implement as part of your *Key Contributor Ready Kit*. Then use Table 3 in the Appendix to fill out aspects of your '*Collaboration Kit*'.

The 21st century will be unfriendly to those superhero types who try to go it alone, ignoring all those around them. In an interdependent workplace, success will belong to those whose knowledge and effort is widely shared.

We have the capacity to make the work of others easier or more difficult, if we've a mind to. Key contributors choose to be those who help their colleagues understand the big picture, complete their projects, and move forward. Less effective organization members hoard information, become locked in fierce competitive struggles with their own colleagues, and try to go it on their own. Contributors establish themselves, not as power brokers, but as people of influence - able to work effectively with a variety of individuals, including those over whom they have little direct authority or control.

1. An Orientation Toward Others

Key contributors take the social initiative and have a participative temperament. They involve others when appropriate, prefer to work and make decisions together with others, and are socially aware and sensitive to the subtleties of interpersonal relationships.

Skill Builders:

☼ Always provide some kind of personal follow-up to any work encounter. Send an e-mail, make a phone call, drop by, and while you're at it, do the more personal version of whatever is standard operating procedure in your company. You'll show that you are someone who really cares about the work of the others in your company.

☼ Seek out opportunities to get to know your coworkers: around the coffeepot, in the elevator, in the parking lot. Ask questions, share your experiences... connect. Your goal is to be that person whom others look forward to bumping into at work. When you connect with other people across the organization, they'll value your work more highly, hold you in higher esteem, and want you on their team! You'll show that you are someone who really cares about the work of your colleagues, *and* you'll develop a reputation as a valuable partner to work with.

Δ Share your ideas with others and ask for input and critique. You don't have to take all the advice, but you just might find a gem. Others will admire your self-improvement efforts, and when they see you have an interest in their opinions, they will tend to include you in their work and share with you what they know.

Δ Determine who you could involve and in what way on projects you have going. Build alliances around good work effort. Let others share in the glory. When they are in a position to reciprocate, they will.

☼ Give some thought to what clubs, associations, or groups you could join that would inspire you in some way, connect you with important others, or make you more effective. Personal connections leverage your power.

2. Responsiveness: Listening, Helping, and Cooperating

Like good caregivers in every avenue of life, those with the capacity for collaboration are skilled at listening and offering feedback. They are able to empathize, connect with others' experience, and take care of the human side of the enterprise. Key contributors are characterized by their inclination to help, to listen, and to cooperate.

Skill Builders:

Δ Look around. If someone needs help or if you have the information that would make another person's job easier, provide it. You'll quickly become known as a 'team player' who has the best interests of the company in mind.

Δ   In a conflict situation, work first to understand the others' point of view. Rather than trying to beat someone down with your own opinions and your own solutions, listen ... really listen, and try to understand what they have to say. You're likely to gather some valuable information once you fully understand their point of view, and your consideration of their opinion and feelings will go a long way toward increasing your influence - even if you ultimately have to 'agree to disagree'.

☼   Make it a point to ask for others' opinions and advice. When you are in a meeting, act as a *gatekeeper*, soliciting the input of those who might not participate spontaneously. You'll be building alliances with those who may have always felt on the outside. Who knows what font of knowledge you might tap into?

☼   Become a mentor for someone junior or less experienced. Teach 'em everything you know. When you send these skilled individuals out into your company (or off to other companies), you will be building allies everywhere. You will have built an extremely wide network of friends and acquaintances who hold you in very high regard. As a result, you have access to lots of people who have the capacity to help you when you need it.

3. Polished People Skills

There is just something about those who achieve the status of key organization contributor that exudes leadership, influence, and well - *charisma*. In everything they say and do, they demonstrate the ability to gain the trust, respect, and confidence of different types of people all over the organization. They have moved away from thinking 'competitive advantage' (especially as it applies to their own colleagues). Instead, they seek a *'collaborative advantage'* with others.

Skill Builders:

☼   Go out of your way to approach people who others find 'difficult'. You'll make allies of employees that may have otherwise been shunned... and you'll have access to their help and information when you (and the company) need it the most.

Δ   Make the most of the *'Listening = Trust'* relationship. It's common knowledge that we are much more likely to listen to the people we trust. But that equation works in the other direction as well. That is, people tend to be more trusting of those people who listen to them. Become known as someone who listens... really listens to the viewpoints of others, and your trust quotient will rise dramatically.

☼   Don't stop yourself from complimenting or appreciating someone when it is deserved. If you show that you respect others' abilities, those who are performing well will want to be on your team.

☼   Laud someone in an e-mail (if they deserve it) and copy your joint boss (or their boss). An employee down the ranks who gets noticed favorably will work harder (at least on your projects), and you will have made an important ally in the process.

The Two Prevailing Orientations Emerge

We believe that these two inclinations – *Personal Initiative* and *Collaboration* – are the initial uplifting factors that underlie the more specific skillsets that we will describe next.

To this point you have had an opportunity to gain an understanding of two prevailing orientations, to assess the degree to which you have balance in your work style in these two areas, and to begin to build some skills in those areas that you would like to develop more fully.

It's now time to look at the more specific skills that define the key organization contributor. In our surveys, four specific skillsets were mentioned, in one way or another, over and over again, as characteristic of those individuals who were the most likely to be successful. We have named these skills: 'Mental Agility' (56% of our respondents identified some form of this skill), 'Action Learning' (48%), 'Visibility' (68%), and 'Boundary Spanning' (54%).

Although the depiction of this model, '*The Phoenix Factor*', implies benefit only to the individuals displaying these attributes, the reason the model is so important is that it is the blueprint for making the entire organization function most effectively.

In the following chapters, we will define in more detail each of the four remaining skillsets, provide you with an opportunity to assess your competence in each area, and provide you with a catalogue of skills, activities, and exercises that you can use to build your ability to make a significant organization contribution.

Chapter Two

Mental Agility: Corporate Quick-Change Artistry

"It's not the strongest of the species that survives, nor the most intelligent, but the one most responsive to change".

- Charles Darwin

Until the beginning of the twentieth century, most people still had the capacity to learn a great percentage of the information available to them. In 1900, a well-educated person could still grasp the existing knowledge in almost every field of science and the arts. In fact, this was what a college education was supposed to provide. Human knowledge was increasing at a rate that a single human brain could still handle. Today, over three hundred thousand new books are produced each year worldwide. One and one-half trillion pieces of paper circulate through U.S. offices each year. Two billion web pages are posted on the Internet. A U.S. government study estimates that the amount of Internet traffic doubles every 25 days. A single weekday edition of the *New York Times* contains more information than the average person was likely to come across in a lifetime in 17th century England. The mental stamina necessary just to cope with the demands of the aerobic workplace - the one that requires so much of our mental, physical, and emotional energy - has increased exponentially.[25]

Mental Agility Is at the Core of Life Inside the New Organization

The technology of the *Industrial Age* gave us mechanical muscle and motorized speed, cotton gins, conveyor belts, tractors, trains, automobiles, and jet engines. The *Information Age* has given us computerized brains and electronic speed. Work is becoming less physical and more mental. We do less with our hands and more with our heads. As new technologies explode and invade our society, as information mushrooms and external demands increase, our lives have gone from a leisurely stroll, or perhaps a jog, to a full-out sprint. High-speed computers, e-mail, Zoom, and all other manner of technological marvel have accelerated the pace at which we receive information and, in turn, how we must act on it. Speed is a key source of competitive advantage. The dollar value of time keeps climbing.[26]

Above all other talents, mental agility - the capacity to function successfully in a change and information-dominant society - is at the core of life inside the new organization. The skill embodies the inclination to think and act quickly and decisively, the ability to respond to change creatively, and the drive to seek out and capitalize on opportunities.

Contributors with mental agility enjoy variety and energetic action. They feel a sense of urgency. They are quick to respond and quick to solve problems. They seem to always be deeply involved in what they are doing and, at the same time, they remain keenly aware of what's happening around them. They are results-oriented and often have several projects going at once. They are resourceful, clear-thinking, alert, observant, perceptive, and quick to grasp ideas. They're fast learners. They have a talent for generating ideas and for seeking novel solutions to problems. They are flexible in work procedures, and they can work comfortably in an unpredictable environment. They brainstorm with others and let their wide-ranging ideas incubate.

What's Different about the Mentally Agile?

Consider this analogy: If you've ever owned a 10-speed bicycle, how many of those ten speeds did you regularly use? Most of us would reply, *"Oh, I don't know ... two, maybe three"*. Contributors with mental agility routinely use all ten mental speeds. They think and act quickly. They shift gears. They speed up when necessary and slow down when advisable. They can attend to and work on more than one thing at a time.

Here's another analogy. Visualize a professional tennis match at the championship level. The player in the return-of-service stance is bouncing back and forth on the balls of her feet, ready to move in any direction to handle whatever comes her way, ready to capitalize on an opportunity or turn the defense of her territory into a winning

---

smash. No championship tennis player stands flat-footed on the baseline, racket hanging down at his side, waiting until the ball is rocketing across the net. Neither does the mentally agile contributor.

Tony Bourdain, former executive chef at New York's celebrated brasserie *Les Halles* and former host of Food Network's series *No Reservations*, says that the religion in the kitchen is *mise en place* - 'your setup' - knowing where everything is in your station, always thinking about what might happen, and being ready for anything. You never know for sure how many people might arrive at any point in time, what might break, and what supplies might not show up. It's chaotic. But the top chefs and top kitchen personnel are indispensable because they are ready for anything in the chaos of the kitchen - because of their preparation and their temperament. Bourdain points out that every kitchen has one genius, someone you turn to when all else fails: the *debrouillard* - the person who gets you out of a jam. When you're really in trouble, say you've run out of prepared hors d'oeuvres during a huge corporate cocktail party, the debrouillard will know about the case of mini-pizzas with frost damage, hidden in the corner of the freezer, and will be the one to go out on a limb and make something memorable out of them.[27]

What Our Surveys Showed

In our surveys, two qualities stood out as the most highly-prized and most often noted: the inclination for *Personal Initiative* and the strategy of *Mental Agility*. These attributes were widely endorsed both by individuals commenting on their own skills as key contributors and by managers searching for top talent to staff their organizations.

When we analyzed the content of our surveys and our interviews, 56% of those surveyed mentioned some aspect of what we have come to call 'mental agility'. Every individual identified as a key contributor was known to display one or more of these skills. Four distinct aspects of mental agility emerged from the data:

1. **Quickness in Thought and Action**: the flexibility to keep pace in a constantly changing work environment

2. **Well-Calibrated Intuitive Skill**: being able to play your hunches and be right most of the time
3. The **Willingness to Act on Calculated Risks**: feeling comfortable taking action, even if all the data is yet to be amassed
4. A **Creative Mind-Set and a Thirst for Innovation**: looking beyond the routine for the ideas that have real breakthrough potential

---

The 80/20 Rule: Finding the High-Impact Activities

Golf fans would love to see Tiger Woods play every PGA tournament, and television producers would like that even more. But Tiger plays fewer tournaments over the course of the year than his PGA brethren. Tiger focuses on the four majors - *The Masters, British Open, U.S. Open,* and *PGA Championship.* Woods's practice regimen and discipline around preparing for the majors is legendary. Could he tally up additional wins and earn even more prize money if he played more? Yes. But that's not the point. Not only are the other tournaments less important for his definition of success, but they can be a distraction in the pursuit of the ultimate goal: winning as many majors as possible.

The tasks and objectives that are required as a part of most business careers are not all glory. The reality is that you can do what you are told at work - and do a good job of it - and still not have success or security in your position. Although you should absolutely seek to meet the objectives set for you at work, you should have no illusion that this is enough. You can meet your goals, get decent performance reviews, even get the occasional raise, and still not have a stellar career. So much of what we do at work is so ordinary that almost any of our peers could accomplish it. In fact, 80% of our tasks offer little chance for distinguishing ourselves. Extraordinary individuals separate themselves from the pack by focusing their effort on the remaining 20% - the tasks that create a bigger impact.

Average employees work solely to exceed preset expectations: achieving more than quota, producing additional reports, or reducing costs by some incremental percentage. This approach rarely creates distinction. The reason is that these successes are considered relatively black or white - either you achieved your objective or you didn't. While you will likely be singled out for *not* meeting the objective, 'exceeded by five percent' will likely only result (on the normally sterile performance evaluation form) as 'met expectations' or, at best, 'exceeded expectations'.

The extraordinary performer takes a different approach. He or she consistently meets objectives and then starts down a different path: to use precious remaining resources to impact the company with objectives that generate the most value. Extraordinarily successful individuals focus on what many people think of as the *work around the edges*, those undefined tasks that no one specifically told them to do but that helped to set them apart. On a day-to-day basis, these tasks may seem like relatively inconsequential things - a marketing manager going on customer visits, a sales manager taking some calls in the customer service center, a manufacturing manager volunteering for a cross-functional quality project. But these activities compound in ways that, over the course of months or years, create exceptional, differentiated results.[28] It is the ability to go beyond merely achieving what others want you to do and breakthrough to deliver unanticipated impact that will give you - and your company - the most return, creating results that can truly distinguish you. The demands of twenty-first-century markets make it necessary for every organization to be populated with high-level performers. There is no longer room for the employee just looking to get by. At the individual level, this means finding a way to let go (at least when opportune) of those low productivity activities in the service of those singular opportunities that present the chance for the biggest payoff for your organization.

1. *Quickness in Thought and Action*

"The final technique for coming up with new business ideas is to maximize one's strategic degrees of freedom".
- Kenichi Ohmae

In the 21st century, business cycles have sped up dramatically. To get an idea of how this works, consider the time it used to take to do something - a business plan, a strategic plan, meeting a customer's request, answering a client's question. Now, reduce that time by one order of magnitude and then halve it. If it used to take you three weeks to craft a business plan, for example, you'd better be able to do it now in one and a half days. Guess what? If you don't, your competitor will. Delay gets deadly in a world of high-velocity change. The outfit that fails to show enough sense of urgency will see its customers disappear. Somebody else will beat them to the market with a newer, better product or service. Speed has become a basic survival skill. And a company can't be fast if its people are slow. It can't adapt rapidly to change if employees resist. The mind-shift that key contributors have made is to think of themselves as accelerators for their organizations. They have a focus on how to increase their organization's operating velocity.

In an age of *instant* everything - instant e-mail, instant messaging, instant news, instant access - we don't have the luxury of finishing every task to the final dotted *i* and crossed *t* before we must move on to the next project. If you're not able to keep several projects going at the same time, all in different stages of completion, and move easily, one to the other, while still keeping the big-picture theme in frame, you're going to have trouble in the new organization.

Key contributors are fast learners and quick to act. They don't wait for all the facts to be in. There just isn't time. They are deeply involved in whatever they are doing and, at the same time, are capable of throwing intense energy into several projects simultaneously. They have highly developed critical abilities and discernment, combining intuitive information with facts in a powerful way. This quickness keeps them results-oriented. This *'functional impulsivity'* represents a method of seizing opportunities in a rapidly changing environment.

In a world dominated by change, *flexibility* might well be the main job qualification - the ability to be highly productive, but if need be, to shift quickly to another point of focus. Even the tradition-bound U.S. Marines have adopted as their 'unofficial' motto: *'Semper Gumby"* – forever flexible. Being flexible allows a key contributor to respond to the moment, to change plans, to put a new twist on a project, or to rearrange a schedule with a minimum of discomfort or delay.

The following quotes about contributors are typical and are drawn directly from our surveys:

> "She seems to thrive on problems to be solved and is always willing to take on something else. She is the individual in this organization that has the most on her plate, and the one who gets the most done".

> "He required very little time to bring him up to speed on projects. His learning curve was the shortest in the division".

> "He could orchestrate a wide variety of projects and seemed to be able to connect them together in ways that made sense".

> "He was seemingly able to throw intense energy in several directions simultaneously".

Twenty-First-Century Minds or Ancient Wisdom?

Some theorists have suggested that what we sometimes refer to as impulsiveness, snap decision making, and a desire to be fulfilled and engaged at every moment, are far from being something new on the block. These traits actually appear to have ancient roots in the early hunting and foraging societies of our primitive ancestors. These quick-reaction inclinations became problematic only when human societies turned agrarian. Farming, and the *Industrial Age* that followed it, both created and demanded predictability. If this is the perfect day to plant, you can't suddenly decide to wander off into the woods. You do what you did last year at this time. When you take your place on an assembly line, you do precisely what you did yesterday. Hunting animals, on the other hand, does not take place on a fixed schedule. Staying flexible, being alert to opportunities, having a willingness to change - the psychological profiles of those ancient hunters who survived - sound a lot like the traits a high-tech start-up company might see in its staff. [29]

"Be quick, but don't hurry."

- John Wooden,
head basketball coach, *UCLA*

Time Means Something Different for Key Contributors

You might expect that those demonstrating mental agility would appear as a blur, jumping from one thing to the next. Not so. In fact, on the contrary, they project a calm demeanor even while they are tackling multiple tasks. Although they often accomplish much more in a day than the rest of us, the mentally agile never *seem* in a hurry. How is this possible?

As our world becomes increasingly fragmented, besides attending to all this information, activity, and potential distraction, we must find a way to tie these diverse elements together in some productive way. This is what most clearly distinguishes those who will thrive and conquer the problems of this new world from those who will be frustrated or disabled by it. The difference between feeling fragmented, confused, chronically anxious, and out of control, versus feeling energized, empowered, creative, and productive, depends on mental agility.

How we conduct ourselves under the press of time has a significant connection to the skill of mental agility. More often than not, most of us tend to work *against* time, hurrying to beat the clock or to squeeze in one more activity. We relentlessly push on, trying desperately to stick to a schedule and follow one activity or train of thought through to what we have determined to be its proper conclusion, resenting each new intrusion, distraction, or additional demand. Time management instructors Diana Hunt and Pam Hait [30] suggest that it is possible to work *with* time - what they refer to as 'non-resistance'. In this way of working, we no longer attempt to force events, and we eliminate much of the effort normally spent trying to *make* things happen, that is, pushing against the grain of time. Key contributors know all too well that, in most of their activity, resisting the natural flow consumes energy and concentration and drains power away. The mentally agile typically do not resist, but relax and allow their experiences to unfold. They trust their intuitive ability to make the right decisions at the time they are required. Invariably, this decisiveness pays off.

Time does seem to have a capricious and variable quality about it. You may have had the experience that athletes '*in the zone*' and others who have experienced a sudden and traumatic life crisis report that time, if not standing still, certainly seems to slow considerably.

On the other hand, it seems that as we get older, time passes faster. The common wisdom holds that this latter experience is simply a matter of scale. The more years you live, the smaller each year seems, so the months start flying by in a discouraging blur. Everyone believes this, even though this view of time is in conflict with what we know - that time is standard, objective - that it doesn't change. Mathematically, those endless summers of our childhood were not even one minute longer than last summer, which seemed to fly by in about two seconds. What's different now is *how you spend your time*. Simply put, you have more routines now, and routines lead to uniformity, which makes it very easy to be oblivious to time. At age 20, life is likely to change in more major ways than at age 50, and the changes help mark the passage of time. Even at 50, a month spent in four different vacation locales will seem slower and loom larger than a regular month at home. Taking more trips, more vacations, or even keeping a diary will foil the time bandit. Looking back on all you did in a week can make the time seem to have expanded. So the mentally agile, with a day and a mind full of interesting and involving activities, seem to have all the time they need. No need to rush. A day full of our more typical routines and activities, un-enlivened by novel things of interest, highly involving tasks, or constant challenge, seems to pass before we feel that we have really gotten anything accomplished.

"Seek out that particular mental attribute which makes you feel most deeply and vitally alive, and when you have found that attitude, follow it".

- William James

The following quotes about contributors are typical and are drawn directly from our surveys:

> "He was one of the ones who could work effectively in our unpredictable environment".

> "He actually seemed to enjoy deadlines. Something about the pressure really energizes him. He usually made the right call and was calm about it, even under extreme pressures".

2. A Well-Calibrated Intuitive Skill

"The intuitive mind is a sacred gift and the rational mind is a faithful servant. We have created a society that honors the servant and has forgotten the gift".

- Albert Einstein

Sometimes There Isn't Time to Think

Psychologists have recently turned their research attention to a phenomenon called *'thin-slicing'* - meaning our ability to understand situations and people based on very narrow "slices" of experience [31] Some individuals are highly skilled at this art. Firefighters, stock traders, cops, and soldiers have honed these skills in ways that frequently and literally save their lives. This skill involves, at least at times, abandoning the standard model of decision making - consciously and deliberately gathering all the facts, sorting through them, and drawing what we take to be a rational conclusion. Instead, in a more 'unconscious' way, it is possible to sort, almost instantaneously, through the available information and draw an immediate judgment. This is done so quickly and so far below our level of awareness that we have no understanding of where our conclusions came from.

The part of our brain that leaps to conclusions like this is called the *'adaptive unconscious'*, and the study of this kind of decision making is one of the most important new fields in psychology. This adaptive unconscious is a kind of giant computer that quickly

---

processes a lot of the data we need in order to keep functioning as human beings. When you walk out into the street and suddenly realize that a truck is bearing down on you, you don't have time to think through all your options. In fact, we have developed a kind of decision-making apparatus that's capable of making very quick judgments based on very little information.

How long did it take you to decide how good a teacher your professor was? A class? Two classes? A semester? In a study exploring student ratings of university professors, psychologists gave students three 10-second videotapes of a teacher, with the sound turned off, and found the students had no difficulty at all coming up with a rating of the teacher's effectiveness. Then they cut the clips back to five seconds, and the ratings were the same. They were remarkably consistent, even when the students were given just two seconds of videotape. Those snap judgments of teacher effectiveness were then compared with evaluations of those same professors, made by their students after a full semester of classes. The ratings were found to be essentially the same. A person watching a silent two-second video clip of a teacher whom he or she has never met will reach conclusions about how good that teacher is that are very similar to those of a student who sat in the teacher's class for an entire semester. That's the power of our adaptive unconscious.[32]

Experienced people use intuition in making a variety of decisions every day. And all of us use our intuition to make the routine decisions we make on a regular basis. Building the power of intuition simply involves building our experience base. Gary Klein, arguably the foremost researcher and thinker in the area of intuition, talks about the skill in this way: [33] Intuition is the way we translate our experiences into judgments and decisions. It's the ability to make decisions by using patterns to recognize what's going on in a situation and to recognize the typical *'action script'* (a routine for responding) with which to react. Once experienced intuitive decision makers see the pattern, any decision they have to make is usually obvious. The more patterns and action scripts we have available, the more expertise we have, and the easier it is to make decisions (in this intuitive way). The patterns tell us what to do and the action scripts tell us how. Without a repertoire of patterns and action scripts we would have to painstakingly think out every situation from scratch. When we are faced with a familiar problem, there is a good chance that the first solution we recognize is going to work. Why? Because in most situations we don't need the best option. We need to quickly identify an acceptable option. Possibly there might be a better one, but if it takes hours to find and evaluate, then there is no practical benefit from searching for the optimal course of action. As the old saying goes, '*Better is the enemy of good enough*'.

Most of us are suspicious of this kind of rapid cognition. We believe that the quality of the decision is directly related to the time and effort that went into making it. That's what we tell our children: "Haste makes waste." "Look before you leap." "Stop and think." "Don't judge a book by its cover." We believe that we are always better off gathering as much information as possible and spending as much time as possible in deliberation. But there are moments, particularly in time-driven, critical situations, when haste does not make waste, when our snap judgments and first impressions can offer better means of making sense of the world. [34] Our key contributors have somehow learned this lesson and have nurtured and sharpened their skill of rapid cognition.

We hear much these days about how rapidly the business world is changing. But while speed, flexibility, and adaptability are the buzzwords in many areas, they don't often seem to be applied to the critical area of making decisions. Ironically, speed, flexibility, and adaptability are precisely the kinds of qualities that can be enhanced by intuitive decision making.

Normally our world requires that decisions be sourced and footnoted, and if we say *how* we feel, we must also be prepared to elaborate on *why* we feel that way. The mentally agile realize that this approach is a mistake, and if we are to learn to improve the quality of the decisions we make, we need to accept the mysterious nature of our snap judgments. We need to respect the fact that it is possible to know without knowing *why* we know and accept that, sometimes, we're better off that way. Contributors have learned to trust their instincts. They don't have time not to.

The following quotes about key contributors are typical and are drawn directly from our surveys:

> "She has the ability to quickly size up a situation and see what needs to be done. Her critical abilities and discernment are remarkable in this way".

> "When there is trouble, he takes care of it without hesitation".

> "She is quick to decide, and direct at getting to the core of the situation".

> "Because of his decisiveness and his intuitive insights, he was a powerful force for change in our group".

3. A Willingness to Act on Calculated Risks

What Constitutes a Risk?

A substantial literature on risk suggests that there are two distinct types of risk takers. One type protects against *'making a mistake'*. These are the planners, the checkers, and the compulsive re-workers. Those characterized by this style have learned to view the world as a dangerous and risky place. Within this worldview, it is crucial for one to be careful and deliberate, to gather tremendous amounts of data before committing to a course of action. Operating in this way may well have had substantial value in the past when the world was plodding and generally predictable and the major risks were well-known. But the world has changed.

Another type of risk taker sees the primary risk in life as *'missing an opportunity'*. These individuals are inclined to act, even before they have all the information that would enable them to make a 'perfect' choice. They're out there, living on the edge, taking chances and often reaping great rewards.

Which strategy is right? Both are - depending on the circumstances, of course. But our organization contributors tend to assume the stance that favors the pursuit of opportunity. In the 21st century organization, relying on the tried and true rarely works to a company's advantage. Organizations that excel in the marketplace are invariably those that are blazing new trails.

In a change-dominant, fast-paced business climate, contributors know that a less considered approach is often an advantage. They know that they must be able to make decisions on the run, and they seek out and seize opportunities. They take on challenges, take *'calculated'* risks, and test themselves against ever-increasing standards of performance. They are described as 'adventurous' and 'tireless in their pursuit of new possibilities', and they repeatedly produce results by seizing the moment. They see the world in terms of possibilities, resources, and potential. They achieve their success through a process that can best be described as *'experimentation as implementation'.*

The mentally agile have one other unique quality that allows them to calculate risks more liberally. They are essentially emotionally disconnected from failure. That is not to say that they are cavalier about failing, but they do seem uniquely able to accept their mistakes as simply something bad that happened, without attaching significant disabling emotion. They ask themselves what went wrong and what it would have taken to succeed. They quickly determine what they need to do to change and to adapt… that is, to *"thrive"*. The story is told of a well-known corporate raider who had failed in a major bid to purchase a particular company. When friends sought to sympathize with him, saying that they were sorry he failed after risking and investing so much, he replied, *"I didn't fail. I may not have bought the company this time, but I sure know how to buy it now"*.

Key contributors, perhaps more so than most of us, see risk - and even 'failure' - as a learning opportunity. The calculated risks they take invariably pay off in surplus learning.

The following quotes about organizational contributors are typical and are drawn directly from our surveys:

> "He could see the opportunity in any roadblock. I can't count the number of times he dug us out of a hole and put us on some new path that worked out much better".

> "I believe his greatest results came from seizing opportunities that presented themselves, rather than just working on what he had been assigned".

> "She was alert to changes and could move quickly to modify her plans or redirect her emphasis as the circumstances required".

> "She is the person in our organization who is the most open to, and curious about, new ways of doing things".

> "He was one of the ones who could work quite comfortably in our unpredictable environment".

4. A Creative Mind-Set and a Thirst for Innovation

"When the rate of change outside an organization is greater than the rate of change inside the organization, the end is near".

- Jack Welch

It's a Numbers Game

Robert Sutton, professor of management science and engineering at Stanford Engineering School,[35] observes: "One unspoken truth about creativity - it isn't about wild talent so much as it is about productivity. To find a few ideas that work, you need to try a lot that don't. It's a pure numbers game. Geniuses don't necessarily have a higher success rate than other creators, they simply do more - and they do a range of different things. They have more successes *and* more failures. That goes for teams and companies too. It's impossible to generate a lot of good ideas without also generating a

---

lot of bad ideas. The thing about creativity is that at the outset, you can't tell which ideas will succeed and which will fail. So the only thing you can do is try to fail faster so that you can move onto the next idea".

Another unspoken truth about creativity: it isn't so much about new ideas as it is about using old ideas in new ways, places, and combinations. Henry Miller said: *"All geniuses are leeches"*.

Competition is now about how much knowledge a company can create. And the contributors are always the ones leading the charge for their companies. They continually seek new challenges and new horizons. They show an openness to new experience and a curiosity that drives them forward. They harbor broad and varied interests and are inclined to experiment in life generally. They tend to prototype new ideas continuously, learning by a process of enlightened trial and error. These individuals feel free to bypass convention, when necessary, as the preferred path to developing imaginative and innovative solutions to problems at hand.

The following quotes about key contributors are typical and are drawn directly from our surveys:

> "He was inspiring to be around because he was always engaging you in some creative conversation. He was brilliant himself, but he could elicit ideas from other people that they would never have come up with on their own".

> "He really gets a kick out of always questioning things, especially the old tried-and-true methods. Usually when we'd get together and do this, we'd come up with some new solution to an old problem that paid big dividends".

> "Whenever I went into her office, she always had several books open on her desk and had something to tell about what she had learned that related to the work we were doing".

"He has extremely broad, varied interests that provide a new slant on things".

"He is extremely innovative. He has the capacity to take creative ideas and make them serve practical purposes".

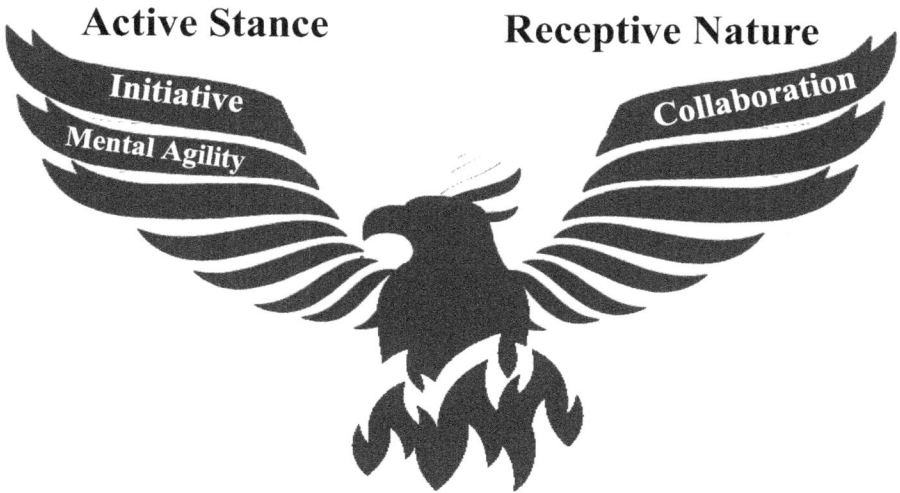

Active Stance   **Receptive Nature**

Initiative   Collaboration

Mental Agility

Are You Mentally Agile?

It's time to test your mental agility. Do you have this strategy of a key organization contributor? Take this short quiz and find out. For each set of descriptors, those on the right of the page and those on the left, check the ones that apply to you. Check as many items as are descriptive of your work style. Your task here is to make as honest an assessment of your skills as possible. The results will help you to understand how natural this ability is for you and, if you choose, guide you to activities and exercises designed to develop the survival skill of mental agility.

☐ I prefer jobs where I have plenty of time to consider all the options.	☐ I enjoy jobs where quick action and decisiveness are required.
☐ I am thoughtful and deliberate in my approach.	☐ I am spontaneous and action-oriented.
☐ I believe in carefully thought-through plans when change is required.	☐ I can change tactics and approaches quickly when circumstances change.
☐ I study any approach thoroughly and immerse myself in the details.	☐ I am considered a fast learner and can grasp ideas and concepts quickly.
☐ I am most successful when I can take one project from start to finish before embarking on another equally demanding task.	☐ I enjoy the stimulation of working on several projects at the same time, and I am usually able to produce good results in this way.
☐ My actions are based on facts and data, carefully considered.	☐ I feel comfortable following my hunches, even when the data are unclear.
☐ I devote most of my intellectual energy to things directly connected to the work I am doing.	☐ I go out of my way to be well-informed about many areas, even those unrelated to my work.
☐ I am interested in learning new information connected to my present skills and abilities.	☐ I can usually see many applications to any new learning.
☐ Most of my energy at work comes from the activities in which I am currently engaged.	☐ I draw energy both from the outside world of people, activities, and things and from the internal world of ideas and impressions.
☐ When I am focused on a task, I am rather single-minded and absorbed in the work.	☐ I am considered alert, observant, perceptive, and resourceful.
☐ I am very careful to avoid making mistakes in my work.	☐ I am always alert to and searching for new opportunities.

☐ I focus on completing the task at hand.	☐ I focus on future possibilities.
☐ Our best efforts are devoted to a careful execution of our current activities.	☐ I communicate options and opportunities and am quick to recognize new possibilities
☐ I work hard to carry out the plan as intended for any project I undertake.	☐ I weigh the pros and cons of any proposal and consider the law of unintended consequences before launching action.
☐ I look at the risks and the likelihood for success before undertaking any project.	☐ I consider the price we pay for *not* taking action as a guide to a decision on a project.
☐ I work hard to perfect my primary talent.	☐ I am always in the process of learning something new
☐ I am known as a solid, steady performer.	☐ I am considered a creative thinker and an "idea person."
☐ I believe in tried-and-true methods.	☐ I am open to and curious about new ways of doing things.
☐ I am interested in learning new information connected to my present skills and abilities.	☐ I can usually see many applications to any new learning
☐ I believe that established policies and procedures represent the best approach to a task.	☐ I have no problem departing from established patterns and going with new ideas
- _____ **Total Boxes Checked**	**+** _____ **Total Boxes Checked**

Our survey results indicate that 56% of the respondents mentioned one or more aspects of what we have come to call *Mental Agility*. Recall that our respondents were either key organization contributors themselves or managers who had the task of selecting employees for positions of prominence in their new organization. They occupied all levels of the organization, from executives to individual contributors. In every case, the respondents were asked to comment on those skills that they believed made employees indispensable to their companies.

Add the numbers in the Totals boxes together, retaining their arithmetic sign. If your score is between -20 and -10, your mental agility is underdeveloped. You may be hampered by too strong an allegiance to routine and predictability - a significant handicap in a change-dominant organizational culture. Your mental agility would be increased by attending to and practicing the exercises and activities in the next section of this chapter.

If your total score is between +10 and +20, your mental agility is likely serving you well. Nevertheless, you may wish to review the exercises and activities in the next section of this chapter to assist you in further developing your mental agility.

Master the Skills of Mental Agility: Become a Corporate Agility Expert

Our surveys with high-impact organizational contributors and the managers who hire them make it clear that one key skill is mental agility. Key contributors have the ability to function successfully in a change-and information-dominant society. This skill is at the very core of life inside the new organization: the inclination to think and act quickly and decisively, the ability to respond to change creatively, and the drive to seek out and capitalize on opportunities. This particular skill comes more naturally to some, but it is a skill that is learnable by everyone.

If you want to add to your mental agility, here are some how-tos to help you sharpen this skill.

As you read through the Skill Builders associated with each aspect of mental agility, circle the symbol beside those you would like to implement as part of your *Key Contributor Ready Kit*. Then use Table 4 in the Appendix to fill out aspects of your *'Mental Agility Kit'*.

1. A Quickness in Thought and Action

Key contributors are fast learners, observant, spontaneous, and alert. They have mastered the art of working comfortably in an unpredictable environment. They can combine intuitive information and facts in a highly effective way. They don't just wait for all the facts to be in ... there isn't time.

Don't Let Perfectionism Get in Your Way

One primary roadblock that stands in the way of your ability to deal successfully with a change-dominant world is perfectionism. We convince ourselves of a need to delay for any number of reasons:
- "I'm not sure how to begin".
- "I work best under the pressure of deadlines".
- "I'll start this project when the one I'm working on is complete".
- "I haven't researched enough".
- "The job is too big".

Regardless of the reasons or rationale behind these obstacles to effective contributions, there is one solution: *start earlier.*

Organization key contributors recognize perfectionism for what it is: collecting information to improve your confidence or to avoid criticism; or waiting for the perfect solution. Anyone with a brain and 100% of the data can make good decisions. The real test - and the real skill of contribution - consists of taking action sooner with a reasonable amount (but not all) of the data. Some studies suggest that the most successful managers are about 65% correct in the decisions they make and the actions they take. Make smaller decisions more quickly. Get started. You can change course and make it perfect along the way.

Skill Builders:

Make the *'luck/planning distinction'*. Tell yourself: I'm going to get into this situation, but I don't expect that planning will make it turn out exactly as I'd expected. I will be careful not to let myself grow too confident and relaxed.

I will expect rapid change. I won't make large irrevocable commitments. I'll stay poised to bail out when I see a change I don't like. Bad luck is not my fault AND my luck will change.

Δ   Pay attention to the 80/20 rule—aka the *'Pareto Principle'*. This well-known dictum is named for Italian economist Vilfredo Pareto (1848–1923). Although it has many applications, the one that is germane here is that 80% of your total productive output derives from a small subset of key activities - probably no more than 20% of your total activity on any given task. In terms of mental agility, this means being able to let go (at least when opportune) of those low productivity activities in the service of those singular opportunities that present the chance for the biggest payoff. This concept is also connected to the idea that in the age of *instant* everything - instant e-mail, instant messaging, instant news, instant access - we don't have the luxury of finishing every task to the final dotted *i* and crossed *t* before we must move on to the next project.

- Look for your high-impact activities (the 20% that will make you remarkable in your organization or that will make a major difference in your organization's performance) and make sure you have addressed these before tackling the remaining 80% (the busywork or low-impact tasks). You'll multiply your impact when you do.
- In a day filled with multitasks, concentrate your efforts on the high-impact 20%. Your day will be more stimulating, you will have a better chance for a big payoff, and when you're basking in the glow of success on several projects, you can always go back and clean up the busywork associated with closing out the other projects.
- Be persistent in your efforts, but be willing to let go of ideas and strategies that are not working. Make sure you have learned *something* and document that learning before moving on. There are no failures if you have learned something valuable along the way.

If you are not able to keep several projects going at the same time, all in different stages of completion, and move easily, one to the other, while still keeping the big-picture theme in frame, you are going to have trouble in the *new* organization.

☼ Practice working on more than one task or project at a time. Be willing to move on to something new, even if the current project is not perfectly complete (as long as you've got the end in sight). Get the 'big picture' outlined so you can fill in the blanks later.

Δ Discover how ideas about one project can apply to another. Not only does this strategy free up your thinking… it energizes your action. Ask yourself:
- "What would be a good mix of projects to take action on today"?
- "How do these different projects or assignments relate to one another"?
- "What learning can I use from one to help me with the others"?

Make use of what's been called the *'Mozart effect'*. In the same way a classical composer constructs a beautiful symphony, create the big themes for your projects. How can one reinforce the other? How can you create an allegro, an adagio, a largo, and still make it recognizable as the same piece of music, each movement with the same central melodic theme? Try out this metaphor in your own work. Keep your big themes in mind for projects and initiatives while you vary your work from day to day. How can you elaborate on these themes in all that you do? As you keep your eye on the big themes, you can easily multitask without losing your focus. Contributors become adept at shifting their attention without losing their leverage. Vary your effort in this way, and you'll multiply your outcomes.

☼ Sometimes (logical thinkers that we are), we are seduced by sequential time. This means that we erroneously assume that we must tackle tasks in sequence and that our days must be scheduled according to the sweep of the clock. Key contributors know better. They reserve their '*prime time*' for the high-impact tasks or for those that require the most creativity. Here's how this works:

- Keep a log of how a day progresses for you. You'll quickly discover that during some parts of the day, you feel highly energized, creative - firing on all cylinders. Other times during the day you feel lethargic, drained, 'out of it'. Keep such a log over a work week, and you'll discover if you are a 'morning person' or a 'late afternoon person'.
- If your thinking and execution efficiency is greatest first thing in the morning - when that second cup of coffee kicks in - schedule your high-demand tasks then. Even if this 'prime time' lasts only an hour or so, you'd be well served to work on critical tasks then. Maybe your greatest thoughts occur only late in the afternoon or evening. When you learn to schedule your critical tasks or work on high-impact projects during your own personal 'prime time', you'll find your output multiplying.

Gear-Shifting

To be truly effective across situations and with a diverse set of people with whom we are in contact on a day-to-day basis, we are called upon to act differently, sometimes from moment to moment - in control at 9AM, a follower at 10, quiet at 11, dominating at noon. All in a day's work... respectful with the boss, critiquing with peers, caring for directs, and responsive to customers. No trickery, no blowing with the wind, just adjusting to the demands of each situation. Key contributors are experts at adaptive gear-shifting.

Skill Builders:

☼ Monitor your gear-shifting behavior for a week at work and at home.

- What switches give you the most trouble? The least? Why?

- Off work, practice gear-shifting transitions. Go from a civic meeting to a run through the park, for example. On the way, between activities, think about the transition you're making and the frame of mind you need to make it work well. Which transitions are the toughest for you? Write down the five toughest. Where do you have a hard time switching?
- Use this information to make a list of discontinuities you face, such as:
    - Leading vs. following
    - Confronting vs. being approachable
    - Relaxing vs. focused work

Write down how each of these discontinuities makes you feel and what you may do that gets you into trouble. For example, you may not shift gears well after a confrontation, or you may have trouble taking charge again after passively sitting through a meeting all day. Create a plan to attack each of the rough transitions.

☼　Interview people who are good at shifting gears.
- Talk to fix-it managers, shut-down managers, or excellent parents.
- Talk to an actor or actress to see how they can play opposing roles back to back.
- Talk to people who have recently joined your organization from places quite different from your own.
- Talk to a therapist, who hears a different trauma or problem every hour.

See if you can figure out some rules for making comfortable transitions.

☼　Control your instant response to shifts. Many of us respond to the fragmentation and discontinuities of work as if they were threats instead of just the way life is. This initial anxious response lasts 45 to 60 seconds, and we need to buy some time before we say or do anything inappropriate. Research suggests that generally somewhere between the second and third thing you think to say or do is the best option. Practice holding back your first response long enough to think of a second and third. Manage your shifts. Don't be a prisoner of them.

2. *A Well-Calibrated Intuitive Skill*

Intuition is something we all have, and smart and savvy organization contributors have relied on it all along. Call it a 'gut feeling', 'instinct', or 'just knowing'. It's a sure guide as to what to do when you don't have all the facts of a situation and you have to make a decision. There have been a number of psychologists and behavioral scientists who have made careers out of researching that phenomenon we call *'intuition'*. Like any muscle, it can be strengthened with exercise. Some people trust their intuition more than others do. But it should be obvious that the capacity to access accurate intuitive insights, and then to trust and act on them, would be of great benefit.

Albert Einstein, Lee Iacocca, Conrad Hilton, and Alexander Graham Bell are among the many successful individuals who have talked openly about the powers of intuition.

> *"The intellect has little to do on the road to discovery. There comes a leap in consciousness, call it intuition, call it what you will, when the solution comes to you, and you don't know how or why".*
> - Albert Einstein

> *"I know when I have a problem and I have done all I can to figure it out, I keep listening in a sort of inside silence until something clicks and I feel a right answer".*
> - Conrad Hilton

> *"We spent almost none of our time studying plans for the mission and almost all of our time learning how to react intuitively to all the 'what-ifs.' Reliance on the intuitive response was the most important part of an astronaut's training".*
> - Edgar Mitchell,
> lunar module pilot of *Apollo 14*

Call it intuitive if you like, but people with years of experience to draw on (or strong gut feelings validated by experience) recognize a pattern of information that might mean nothing to others. The novice would have to attack the problem by considering analytically many possible solutions; the experienced person sees a possible solution immediately - not the best solution, maybe, but one that works. Management books may say look at all the options, identify evaluation criteria, weigh the options numerically, and see which option has the highest score. Everybody talks that approach. The fact is, hardly any successful and productive person uses it. Intuitive decisions are actually a sophisticated form of *pattern recognition*. Analytic problem solving is fine - if you've got all the time in the world. More and more often now, we don't. Those who become key contributors know this.

In a fascinating study of individuals who were widely recognized by their friends and relatives as incredibly lucky, author Max Gunther[36] discovered a form of intuition he calls *'the hunching skill'*. Although it seems mysterious, intuition can be explained in rational terms. Better yet, there is compelling evidence that it can be learned. Where does intuition come from? Psychologists believe they have the answer.

In essence the theory is this: intuition is a conclusion that is based on perfectly real data, on objective facts that have been observed, efficiently stored and logically processed by the mind. The facts on which intuition is based, however, are facts that are not necessarily consciously known. They are stored and processed on some level of awareness just below or behind the conscious level. That is why intuition comes with that peculiar feeling ('gut feeling') of almost, but not quite knowing. It is something that you think you know, but you don't know how you know it. [37]

Intuition is built on data you can't quite pull up to the conscious level. Facts you can't list, can't identify, can't exhibit, to prove the reliability of your conclusion to anybody else, or indeed even to yourself. But the use of intuition is a skill well known to our mentally agile organization contributors.

Consider this example: A man and his female colleague go to a business conference. A friend later asks them what the conference was like. The man reports: *"Well, Bill and Mary were there, and Ed and Neal. We talked about the strategic initiatives. Here's the ideas we came up with. I've created a spreadsheet to share. We also got to meet all the new hires"*. But the woman reports: *"It was nice to see a lot of these people again and to meet the new hires, but there was some sort of stiffness in the air. I had this feeling we were all competing with each other. You know, showing off about how well we have done and how fast our respective groups have come together. Most of the new hires, though, seemed really glad to be on board"*.

The man restricted himself to hard facts. The woman dealt with soft facts - *intuition stuff*. If somebody challenges them to produce evidence that their observations are accurate, the man will, of course, have the more provable case, by far. The woman may not be able to produce any proof at all. Yet if this man and woman are later called on to make some difficult decision involving somebody at the conference, or the company more generally, it is likely that the woman's intuition will be the more reliable. Some people trust their intuition more than others do. But it should be obvious that the capacity to access accurate intuitive insights, and then to trust and act on them, would be of great benefit. Intuition is something we all have, and smart and savvy key contributors have relied on it all along.

Are there steps you can take to sharpen this 'intuitive muscle'? There are!

Skill Builders:

U   Let's listen again to Max Gunther.[38] Ask yourself a series of self-questions that allow you to tune in more completely to this set of below-conscious-level data. "What do I feel about this situation"? The feeling replies, "Uneasy? Worried"? You ask the feeling to define itself more narrowly. "Worried about what"? "It's a feeling of things getting out of control. Like I'm trying to hold something up, but it's starting to collapse around me". "What's the worst part of this collapse"? "It's something about my boss. I have a hunch he doesn't really support this project even though he's given me the go-ahead". "Lack of support in what way"? "What has he not done"? And so on … Don't ask for reasons or explanations, just for more and more details about the feelings. Mentally agile contributors, who are experts at using their intuition, go through some such process at every decision-making point in their lives.

☼   Collect soft facts along with the hard. Soft facts are feelings, impressions, or to use a word from the 1960's, *'vibrations'*. Hard facts - the overt, the objective - seem more real to many people. Many restrict themselves to observing hard facts alone and dismiss all other observations as irrelevant, trivial, or unreliable. If you habitually restrict yourself in this way, your intuition doesn't get any exercise. And we know that intuition improves with practice.

☼   To become good at mining your intuition, you have to practice it every day, and in every situation. Keep forcing yourself to perceive more than you see. Keep asking yourself for the 'vibrations' here. *"What do I feel"?* Most of the judgments we make in daily living, whether we like it or not, require us to use our intuition constantly through decisions big and small.
- "Should I take this job"?
- "Are the R&D people telling the truth when they say all the bugs have been worked out"?
- "Will my boss be angry if I …"?

Key contributors often turn out to be people whose intuition at life's major and minor crossroads is trustworthy.

☼   Learn to assess the data base. Intuition usually comes as a strong feeling that such-and-such is true. Ask yourself how solid the underlying database is for this intuition. Obviously you don't know what facts this intuition is based on, and you have no hope of knowing them since they are beyond your conscious awareness. But what you *can* do is ask whether these facts might exist. Ask yourself: *"Is it conceivable that I have gathered a pool of data on this situation without realizing it"? "Have I been in a position to gather these facts"? "Even though I can't see these facts, is it reasonable to think that they are there"?* If the answer to these questions is *'Yes',* and the intuition feels strong - go with it. [39]

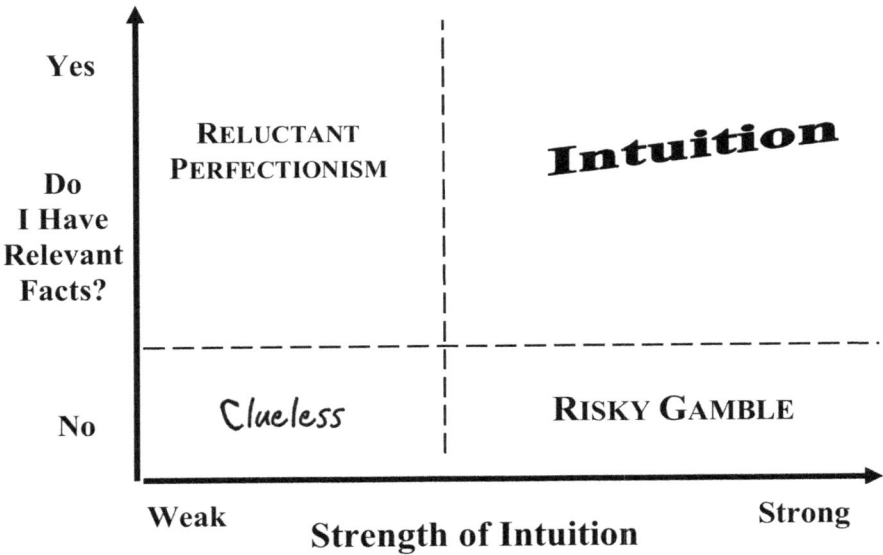

Yes

Do I Have Relevant Facts?

RELUCTANT PERFECTIONISM

Intuition

No

Clueless

RISKY GAMBLE

Weak   **Strength of Intuition**   **Strong**

☼   Try your intuition out with small decisions first. As you become more skilled at trusting your judgment, your 'gut feeling', gradually expand your powers of intuition to bigger things. You won't be disappointed, and you will greatly leverage your time and energy.

☼   Build your intuitive skill and confidence in your ability. As you begin to feel more comfortable, you can tap into your intuition in more significant areas of your life.

☼   Don't bother with *intuitive feel* where there is no possibility that this intuition could have welled up from some hidden pool of facts inside you. There are no facts about the results of a future lottery drawing or about the random alignment of cogs at some future moment inside a slot machine. Any such 'intuition' should be dismissed as untrustworthy. Intuition is only as good as the sum of past experiences that produce it. You can trust your intuition only if you've had experience in the situation it deals with. When your intuition comes, always ask yourself whether the underlying facts could be there - just below your conscious awareness. Ask whether you could have absorbed the data about the situation.[40]

☼　　Never fall back on your intuition to avoid work. First, find out all you can about the situation in which you need to make a decision. Steep yourself in it. Doggedly seek the facts of it. Try to reach your decision first based on hard data. If you can't, then fall back on your intuition - but only then.

☼　　Never confuse intuition with hope. If your intuition tells you something is true and you badly *want* it to be true, regard your intuition with suspicion. A lot of bad intuition is just strong wishing in disguise. When intuition and hope are churning about in the mind and the gut, they feel confusingly alike.

☼　　Don't smother your intuition by trying to figure it out. This is a key lesson. Sit quietly and relax and, as far as possible, suspend the intellectual process. Don't try to analyze anything. Don't intellectualize it. Don't figure it out. Don't say it must be. Don't say X is true, therefore Y must be true also. Just ask yourself what you feel about the situation and let that feeling float up freely. A feeling about a situation always contains vastly more information than could have been figured out intellectually. The feeling is the stored total of the situation as the mind and body have been experiencing it. It is an enormously rich mass of facts and impressions, many of them without words to label them. If you insist on always approaching problems and decisions in a strictly analytical way, dealing with only those parts that can be described in words and related to consciously known facts, you are imposing very great restrictions on yourself. This is like going out to prospect for oil with a drill that will go only ten feet deep. Most of the riches lie deeper. [41]

☼　　Take up poker. It's a great way to sharpen intuition and learn how to respond to subtle cues.

Δ　　Ask to be rotated through a variety of jobs. Serve on task forces. Soak up as much secondhand experience as you can find from the old-timers who are successful and using their gut instincts to solve problems.

By the way, cultivating your intuition also affords you the opportunity to pick up on subtle cues that bosses and influential peers are constantly giving off - cues that when responded to, pay big dividends in recognition and a feeling of comfort by the 'big fish' when they deal with you.

Priming Your Unconscious

New York University psychologist John Bargh did a fascinating series of research studies based on the concept of 'priming' the *adaptive unconscious*.[42]　To get a feel for one such experiment, imagine a university professor has asked you to come and see him in his office. You walk down a long a corridor and enter a room where you are confronted with the following test.　On a sheet of paper in front of you is a list of five-word sets. Your task is to make a grammatical four-word sentence as quickly as possible out of each set. It's called a "scrambled sentence test."

1. him was worried she always
2. from are Florida oranges temperature
3. ball throw the toss silently
4. shoes give replace old the
5. he observes occasionally people watches
6. be will sweat lonely they
7. sky the seamless gray is
8. should now withdraw forgetful we
9. us bingo sing play let
10. sunlight makes temperature wrinkle raisins

That seems straightforward, right? Actually, it wasn't. After you finish the test, believe it or not, you would have walked out of the office and back down the corridor more slowly than you walked in. With that simple test, the way you behaved was affected. How? Well, look back at the list. Scattered throughout are certain words such as 'worried', 'Florida', 'old', 'lonely', 'gray', 'bingo', and 'wrinkles'. You thought that you were just taking a language test. But, in fact, what was also going on was making the big computer in your brain, your *adaptive unconscious*, think about the state of being old. It didn't inform the rest of your brain about its sudden obsession. But it took all this talk of old age so seriously that by the time you finished and walked down the corridor, you acted old. You walked slowly. This experiment shows just how much goes on behind that locked door of our adaptive unconscious.

The effects of priming aren't trivial. Two Dutch researchers did a study in which they had groups of students answer 42 fairly demanding questions from the board game *Trivial Pursuit*. Half were asked to take five minutes beforehand to think about what it would mean to be a 'professor' and write down everything that came to mind. Those students got 56% of the questions right. The other half of the students were asked to sit and think about 'soccer hooligans'. They ended up getting just 42% of the *Trivial Pursuit* questions right. The 'professor' group didn't know more than the 'soccer hooligans' group. They weren't smarter or more focused or more serious. They were simply in a smart frame of mind, and clearly associating themselves with the idea of something smart - like a professor - made it a lot easier, in that instant after a trivia question was asked, to blurt out the right answer. The difference between 56% and 42% is enormous.[43]

The results from these experiments are quite instructive. They suggest that your unconscious can set the stage for allowing you to behave and to think at your best or at your worst.

Skill Builders:

☼   What are the possibilities if you 'prime' your *adaptive unconscious* with smart thinking each day? This may well allow your mental agility the structure it needs to roam freely and to create new ideas. Consider a brief quiet time at the beginning of each day - or any time you need rejuvenating - to put yourself in a 'frame of mind' that is primed for mental agility. Imagine yourself being wildly successful, creative, self-assured, and productive. Experiment. See what happens.

3. A Willingness to Act on Calculated Risks

Sometimes taking action involves pushing the envelope, taking chances, and trying bold new initiatives. Research tells us that successful managers have made more mistakes in their careers than those who were not so successful. The trick is to use mistakes and failures as chances to learn. Nothing ventured, nothing gained. Remember, the professional baseball player who wins the batting title each year rarely has a batting average above .400. This translates into failing to get on base six out of every ten times at bat. But remember... organization contributors depend on *calculated* risk. 'Calculated' means you don't blast into a major task just to prove your boldness.

Reluctance is usually driven by anxiety. And anxiety is nothing more than false fear. Anxiety is the reason you over-study opportunities and then fail to take action until it's too late.

Skill Builders:

☼ Make a list of the last 20 things that you were anxious about. How many of them actually occurred? If you had ignored that anxiety, how much more could you have accomplished?

☼ Up your risk comfort. Start small so you can recover more quickly. Go for small wins.

☼ Review each step to see what you did well and what didn't work. Capture the learning from every experience. You're building a huge and valuable data base.

☼ Challenge yourself. See how creative you can be in taking action in a number of different ways. Develop a philosophical stance toward mistakes and failures. Most innovations fail, most proposals fail, most change efforts fail, and the initial solutions to complex problems often do not work. Contributors aren't disabled by their momentary failures.

Δ   Fail fast so you can succeed sooner. Allow yourself to let go of a once promising idea that just isn't working anymore. Months and even years can slip away as everyone labors to keep a doomed project from dying. Meanwhile, much brighter projects lay dormant, with no one to give them any attention. Your power (and your indispensability) will come from directing your activities to the high-payoff projects, right?

Δ   Learn to 'calculate' risks. Mentally agile organization contributors seem to calculate risks by the answers to three specific questions. Most of us stop after answering the first two questions. The true fruit - and often the impetus for action - lies in the answer to the third. Ask yourself:

1. *"What are my odds for success"?* This may be a good place to tap into your intuition.
- "How likely is it that my efforts will succeed"?
- "Are there still things that I can do to up my chances for success"?
- "Would my efforts be aided by involving some specific other people? Who else should I involve"?
- "Who in my organization can I enlist to support my plans"?
- "What are the primary obstacles that stand in my way"?

2. *"What is my exposure if things go wrong"?*
- "Is this a career-ending or career-limiting decision if it fails"?
- "How long will it take me to recover from a failure here"?
- "How key is this decision to how I am, or how I will be, viewed in the organization if things go wrong"?

- "Have I made contingency plans for how to get around these obstacles"?

... and now for that most important third question...

3. *"What is the price I (we) pay for doing nothing here"?*
- "Am I satisfied with things as they stand now"?
- "What opportunities are being lost now"?
- "Where will I (we) be a year from now (or five years from now) if I (we) continue on our present path"?

Although the answers to the first two questions can help evaluate the risks and benefits of any course of action, typically the answer to this third question is the answer that gets us off dead center. Answers to the odds-for-success and exposure-if-things-go-wrong questions often offset each other in a way that keeps us stuck. Sometimes the answer to the third question, *"What's the price of doing nothing"?* is what encourages us to move forward.

Risk-to-Reward Ratio

'Calculated' risks are those in which the risk-to-reward ratio is the greatest. When the degree of risk is low, the likelihood of a large payoff is also limited. When you are hesitant to take any but the most

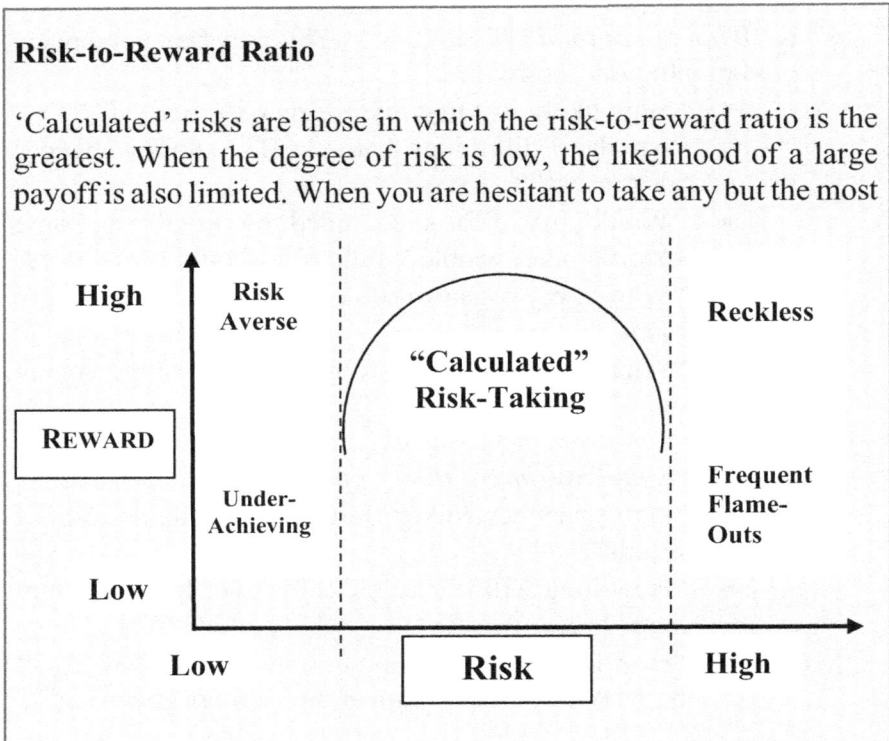

---

minimal risk, the danger is that of setting goals that are too low - underestimating your ability and underperforming. If you never fail at anything you attempt, chances are you are underestimating your ability. Likewise, when the degree of risk is high, the total probability of a large payoff is also often minimal. If you are always at the upper extremes of risk in your business and personal life, your chances of repeated success are low and you may be continually overestimating your talents and abilities - and experiencing spectacular failures, the kind that draw (unwanted) attention. Organization key contributors' 'calculations' effectively balance the dynamic between risk and reward and maximize the chances for a big payoff.

A tremendous amount of research has been carried out on calculated risk and the opportunities for reward. Consider the strategies people devise for competing in a simple ring-toss game. A peg is set at one end of a corridor. Distances are marked from the peg along with corresponding increasing score values - the farther from the peg one stands, the higher the payoff when a ringer is made. Competitors are given three rings. They may stand at any distance from the peg and attempt to throw their rings over the peg. The object of the game is to earn the most points possible with three ring tosses. Of course, it is possible to stand directly over the peg, ensuring that every ring will score. However, the score for each successful ringer using such a strategy is very low. Competitors who stand at the far end of the gradient stand little chance of making a ringer. However, in the unlikely event that they do manage to get their ring over the peg, the corresponding score is very high. The most frequent 'winners' in the ring-toss game tend to adjust their strategy as they make their attempts, finally ending up near the middle of the gradient - optimizing their risk-to-reward ratio and invariably earning the highest scores over the three tosses.

♘ Consider *'risk-spooning'* [44]. The lucky among us don't take crazy goofy risks, but they don't avoid risks at all costs either. Take risks in carefully measured *'spoonfuls'*. Don't be luck neutral. Assess the risk/reward ratios, seek out risks, but start small.

☙ Add in *worst-case analysis*. Ask yourself, 'What's the worst that could happen and how will I protect myself if that occurs'?

☼ How can you optimize your risk-to-reward ratio with your projects at work? Ask yourself: "Which projects are doable (albeit with some considerable effort) and stand the greatest chance of paying big rewards for the organization"?

☼ Order your projects from least to most in terms of difficulty. Rank them again in terms of payoff. Devote your greatest effort to those at the midrange of the risk-to-reward gradient. Key contributors seem to continually seek new challenges and new horizons. They have an openness to new experience and curiosity. Their interests are broad and varied. They are inclined to experiment in life generally. They prototype new ideas continuously, learning by a process of enlightened trial and error. These individuals feel free to bypass convention, when necessary as the path to developing imaginative and innovative solutions to problems at hand.

4. A Creative Mind-Set and a Thirst for Innovation

Researchers who study the subject tell us that creativity isn't about wild talent so much as it is about productivity. To find a few ideas that work, you need to try a lot that don't. It's a pure numbers game. Geniuses don't necessarily have a higher success rate than other creators; they simply do more - and they do a range of different things. They have more successes *and* more failures. That goes for teams and companies too. It's impossible to generate a lot of good ideas without also generating a lot of bad ideas. The thing about creativity is that at the outset, you can't tell which ideas will succeed and which will fail. So the only thing you can do is try to fail faster so that you can move onto the next idea - the one that will likely succeed.

Learning on the Fly

In David Bayles and Ted Orland's wonderful little book *Art and Fear: Observations on the Perils (and Rewards) of Artmaking,*[45] there is a clever anecdote about the value of output in the creative process.

A ceramics teacher announces on opening day of the semester that he is dividing the class into two groups. All those on the left side of the studio will be graded solely on the *quantity* of the work they produce - 50 pounds of pots rates an 'A', 40 pounds a 'B', and so on. All those on the right side of the studio will be graded solely on their work's *quality*. They need to produce only one pot - albeit a perfect one - to get an 'A'. As it turned out, at grading time, the works with the highest quality were all produced by the group being graded for quantity. It seemed that while the 'quantity group' was busy churning out piles of work and learning from the process, the 'quality group' sat, theorizing about perfection and, in the end, had little creativity to show for their efforts.

Skill Builders:

☼   Hold a *'forgive and remember'* policy with regard to failure. Forgive, but remember what has been learned. Successful cold-call sales professionals believe that each *'No'* is one step closer to the ultimate *'Yes',* so they are not dissuaded by rejections, but keep relentlessly plowing forward to the next call, mastering their pitch in the process. The quicker you get out there and get some feedback on your efforts, the closer you are to success.

Δ   After completing any task, ask yourself whether the results can be used in any other way - to solve a different problem, to meet someone else's need, or to create a new and profitable line of business. This makes any experience - success or failure - an opportunity to move forward in a powerful way.

Δ   Always be on the lookout for "How can I use that"? When you see a movie, go to a training event, read a book or an article - any dramatic experience (jury duty?) - ask yourself, "How does this relate to my current project"?

Δ   Ask what parallels your problem. How can you use information from parallel systems to help you now? The developer of *Velcro*, Swiss inventor George de Mestral, got the idea when he noticed how cockleburs attached to his wool socks after a walk in the fields near his home.

☼   Encourage yourself to do quick experiments and trials and look at failures as having useful applications. *Post-it Notes* were actually the result of an error in a glue formula - glue that didn't stick very well and could be easily removed... and the rest is history.

U   The ZigZag path.[46] Lucky people not only allow themselves to be distracted, they invite distraction. They are not straight-line livers - they are 'zigzaggers'. Unlucky people stick to the path, even when it's going downhill. Long-range plans shouldn't necessarily be taken too seriously. If something better comes along, you should be ready to abandon your old plan without regret. Use long-term plans for general guidance as long as they seem to be taking you where you want to go. Lucky people follow new things that *feel right*. You never know from which direction your lucky breaks will come. When they drift into reach, grab them!

Δ   Ask, "Why not"? You'll be surprised at the new (and creative) directions this line of thinking leads to.

Δ   Ask others for input. Even if you think you have a solution, ask some others for input to make sure. One common mistake is to search in only parallel systems because (we wrongly assume) only people who have the same experience would know. Mentally agile contributors look for parallels, associations, and solutions in a wide variety of contexts. This strategy also helps to free you from the shackles of the familiar. When *Motorola* wanted to find out how to process orders more quickly, they went not to other electronic firms, but to *Domino's Pizza* and *Federal Express*.

Δ   Ask stupid questions. There are no stupid questions in the search for a creative response.

Δ   Invite people who have no idea of what the technical issue is into your problem-solving meetings. These people are not hampered by the blinders of experience. They are free to ask questions that may shake the group loose from the deadly *'That's the way it's always been done around here'*.

Δ   Cultivate slow learners of the organizational code. They are not so bound by *'how things are supposed to be around here'*.

Think in New Ways

It was Albert Einstein who pointed out that problems cannot be solved at the same level of thinking in which they were created. If you always do what you've always done, you'll always get what you've always gotten. New thinking patterns, energy, and insights will not only solve the current dilemma; they will move organizations and society itself beyond one entire class of problems to a 'much better class of problems'. Unfortunately many of us have been conditioned to be restrained, narrow, focused, hesitant, cautious, conservative, afraid to err, and unwilling to make fools of ourselves. One process to increasing creativity is to lift those restraints. Think: *'new and improved'*.

☼ Say *'Yes'* and go with the flow. The mentally agile understand that there is a structure that allows creativity to work most effectively. Consider an improvisational comedy group. They get up on stage without any idea whatsoever of what character they will be playing or what plot they will be acting out, take a random suggestion from the audience, and then without so much as a moment's consultation, make up a scene from scratch. Sometimes what is said and done doesn't quite work. But often it is hilarious, and the audience howls with delight. Here is a group of people up on stage without a net, creating a play before our eyes.

Improvisational comedy is a wonderful example of the kind of thinking that mental agility is all about. It involves making very sophisticated decisions on the spur-of-the-moment without the benefit of any kind of script or plot. The truth is that improv isn't random and chaotic at all. To improvise is an art form governed by a series of rules. One of the most important of the rules that makes improv possible is the idea of *agreement*. A very simple way to create a story through improvisation is to have the characters accept everything that happens to them and build on that. Good improvisers accept all offers made, which is something no normal person would do. Normally we are too caught up in our critical thinking to accept the fact that we can go with the flow of our ideas and make snap decisions on the fly. The mentally agile reverse this rule and accept all ideas and suggestions that come their way and see where they lead.

If you create the right framework, all of a sudden, engaging in the kind of fluid, effortless, spur-of-the-moment thinking that makes for mental agility becomes a lot easier. Allowing other people to operate without having to explain themselves constantly turns out to be a lot like the rules of agreement in improv[47]. It enables creativity. The mentally agile learn to trust their instincts in this way. They know they don't have time not to.

☼ Remove your constraints to creativity. Worried about what others might think or that you won't be able to defend your idea? By its very nature, being creative means throwing uncertain things up for critique or review. Narrow perspective? Most comfortable with your technology and profession? Being creative is looking everywhere for connections and parallels.

Δ Let go of the past. Many busy people rely too much on solutions from their own history. They rely on what has happened to them in the past. They see a sameness in problems that isn't always there: *'Because of___ I have always___'* or *'Usually I___'* Think and act differently, try new things, break free of your restraints. Look under new rocks. *'If I don't solve this problem in the same old way, what might I do differently'?* Become aware of how often (and how unnecessarily) old patterns of behavior encourage us to go through life semi-asleep. Wake up and be alert enough to respond to the impulses and impressions around you. Then life can become new again, and you improve your chances of responding positively to the unusual, which often disguises a new opportunity.
- Walk down the stairs with the opposite foot forward from usual.
- Consciously sit in a different place from usual at the dinner table, in meetings, in restaurants - and get a different perspective on things.

113

- Observe and question your routines, changing them when possible, just as an exercise in creative thinking.

☼ Act on your curiosity. Stretch your brain in new directions and be open to new experiences. It's an investment that ultimately pays off and makes everything easier.

☼ Just tell yourself you want to be more creative. This first step to becoming creative is easy, according to creativity experts. This simple self-instruction seems to increase your tolerance for ambiguity, your mental flexibility, your openness to new experiences, and your intolerance for novelty. It often provides a boost of energy. You have a great idea for a new project and suddenly you go from feeling lethargic to being able to pull an all-nighter. When you observe them, you see that the mentally agile seem to have this kind of energy readily at their disposal.

☼ Practice a daily *'openness hour'*. Listen to music, read things that are outside of your normal interests, learn a new language, do crossword puzzles, travel to new places, or take up a hobby that requires you to stretch your mental muscle. Take a class, maybe even something in your area that you can get a certificate for (thereby increasing your visibility as well).

Revamp the Tried-and-True

Another unspoken truth about creativity is that it isn't so much about new ideas as it is about using old ideas in new ways, places, and combinations. For decades companies held to the dictum *'not invented here'*. If it didn't come from the geniuses in our company, how could it be any good? Today a better maxim might be *'stolen proudly from somewhere else'*. The hard truth is that there are no new ideas. There are only new applications and smart tweaks on old ideas.

Δ   Be observant. Look for new ways to apply standard learnings. It has been said that 'There is nothing new under the sun'. Every creative idea is just some reworking or new application of an old idea. Try to discover more (or related) uses for any work product. This will multiply your impact.

☼   Think out loud. Many people don't know what they know until they talk it out. Find a good sounding board and talk to him/her to increase your understanding of a problem or technical area. Talk to an expert in an unrelated field. Talk to the most irreverent person you know. The goal is not necessarily to get his or her input, but rather help in figuring out what you know.

Δ   Unearth creative ideas. Creative thought processes do not follow formal rules of logic, where one uses cause and effect to prove or solve something. The most important rule of creative thought is to change the concepts. Imagine what you are working with were something else: 'What if this team were a car that needed maintenance? What would I do'? 'What if this project were my child? How would I encourage her to develop and learn'?

Δ   Generate ideas without judging them initially. Try to come up with as many ideas as you can before you begin to evaluate them (it's called *'brainstorming'*). Spend some time on this. After you have exhausted all the concepts you can think of, wait a while and keep thinking. Ask more questions before jumping to solutions. Once you've come up with every idea you can think of, throw them all out and wait for others to come to you. Very often the most creative brainstorms occur just after this quiescent period.

Δ   Jump from one idea or project to another. Ask yourself how concepts from one task can apply to another.

Δ   Look at the problem from the reverse direction. What can you learn? 'We need to get this information on the new strategic initiative out to everyone in the organization so that they understand it'. 'But what if we wanted to keep it a complete secret from everyone? What would we do'? You'll be surprised at the new and creative approaches this generates.

Δ   Look for parallels far removed from the problem at hand. Margaret Wheatley, former professor of management at Brigham Young University and currently a principal in her own consulting firm, wrote one of the most influential management books of the recent past - *Leadership and the New Science: Discovering Order in a Chaotic World* [48] - by immersing herself in a study of quantum physics, chaos theory, and biology. In so doing, she was able to find parallels and draw powerful insights about how to transform the way we organize work and people within corporations.

Δ   Ask 'What's missing'? or 'What's not here'?

Δ   Use both/and thinking because it's more powerful than either/or thinking. Both/and thinking is inclusive and empowering. 'How can we meet our deadlines *and* have a quality product'? ... not ... 'We can either meet the deadline or take more time and have a quality product'. *'How-to'* thinking also changes the frame of reference from simply describing a problem to beginning to think through action – a solution.

Δ   Put problems into a visual format. Storyboard your ideas, use mind mapping, translate your concepts into chart or graphic form. Very often a new modality will reveal additional insights.

Δ   Going to extremes helps. Adding every condition and worst-case scenario sometimes will suggest a different solution. Taking the present state of affairs and projecting into the future will sometimes indicate how and where the system will break down.

☼   Sleep on it. Take periodic breaks whether stuck or not. This allows the brain to continue to work on the issue by putting it on the back burner and allowing ideas to percolate. Most breakthroughs occur when we're 'not thinking about it'. There are also numerous accounts of breakthrough ideas coming to scientists and other concept workers literally during their dreams.

Expand Your Creativity

Rigid or narrow beliefs hold us back. The Hopi Indians in the southwest have one word for snow, because they rarely see it. The Inuits of Alaska have 24 four different words for 24 different kinds of snow conditions. A Hopi would not survive in Alaska with just one snow concept. Their experience with the concept of snow is not rich enough to give them the information they need to survive in an Alaskan environment. Our accumulated experience unknowingly creates boundaries for our thinking, especially when some new ideas are called for.

☼   Think outside your belief boundaries when thinking about a problem situation. You don't have to give your beliefs up; just turn them off for a while when you are thinking about a problem or challenge. There are several books that offer assistance in problem-solving strategies: Edward De Bono's *Six Thinking Hats* (and any of his other works), Tony Buzan's *Use Both Sides of Your Brain,* and Gerald Nadler and Shozo Hibino's *Breakthrough Thinking* - all can provide useful strategies for freeing up the thinking process.

☼   Exercise your brain. Crossword puzzles, mental puzzle materials, and logic games can all work to keep your thinking sharp. For a real treat and a chance to exercise your thinking process, pick up William Poundstone's *How Would You Move Mount Fuji?: How the World's Smartest Companies Select the Most Creative Thinkers.*

A New Kind of Critical Thinking

The mentally agile seem to think differently than the rest of us about opportunity and change. For example, consider most people's typical response to the introduction of a new idea in a meeting or the implementation of a new work process. Imagine a continuum of possible responses from *'The worst idea I've ever heard'* to *'The best idea I've ever heard. I agree 100%'.*

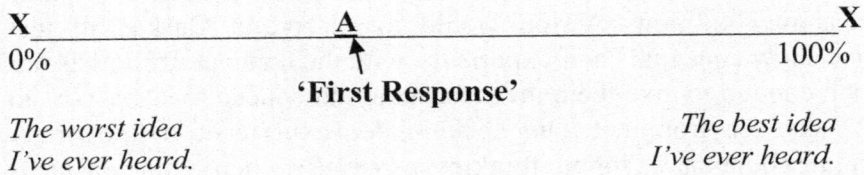

X   A   X

0%   ↑   100%

'First Response'

The worst idea   *The best idea*
I've ever heard.   *I've ever heard.*

For many of us, our first response to any new idea or initiative falls somewhere near the **'A'** on this continuum. Why? Why is our first response usually so critical? Part of the answer is that we are trained from an early age in *'critical thinking'*. 'Critical' can mean reasoned and logical. In this way, critical thinking can be a useful aspect of judgment when our intention is to stay within certain existing boundaries and conform to a predetermined set of guidelines. But critical thinking of this type is the enemy of breaking new ground or finding a new path. And for the person offering up the new idea, 'critical thinking' in response to their idea feels like the other definition of 'critical' - finding fault with. They usually don't feel that others have given them a 30% vote of confidence. More likely it feels like everyone is lining up to put their **'X'** at the 0% end of the continuum.

A friend of mine refers to this as 'quail hunting': getting out the shotguns and shooting down any idea before it has a chance to take flight. What are the consequences for an individual, a team, or an organization if every time someone offers up a new idea, others begin to criticize it? Fresh ideas - or at least their expression in meetings - are likely to dry up. Mentally agile organization contributors know that there is a more productive first response to any new initiative. Key contributors tend to apply this strategy both in evaluating their own ideas and when they interact with others.

The first task is to at least recognize the 30% value of the idea or initiative. This is accomplished by what is called 'stretching for the pluses'.

'Stretching for the Pluses'

X_____A_____X

0%   **'First Response'**   100%
The worst idea   *The best idea*
I've ever heard.   *I've ever heard.*

Stretching for the pluses when interacting with someone around their new idea sounds like this...

> "Here's what I like about the idea ..."
> "That could work because ..."
> "What I see as especially useful about this is ..."

The importance of this way of reacting, whether it is self-talk about your own idea or feedback to someone else, is that it captures the value of the idea and encourages the idea-giver to continue. It doesn't mean you are jumping on board with a half-baked idea. It simply means you are pausing your 'critical' thinking for the time it takes to tease out all the value that exists in the idea as it currently stands.

Δ   Search for ways you can use these lead-ins in interacting with others over the next few weeks. See if this makes a difference in the quality of the interaction and the output of creative ideas among your colleagues. Our guess is that new ideas, and the energy to produce them, will multiply in your group.

Building to the Threshold of Acceptability

Now imagine another point on this same dimension - the point where you can get fully behind the idea and work to make it successful. Let's call this the *Threshold of Acceptability*. This is the point at which, although you might not agree with the idea 100%, you feel that you can get behind it and support it.

'Stretching for the Pluses'   **'Building'**

⟶   ⟶

X ———————————— **A** —————— **B** ——————————— X

0%   'First Response'   'Threshold of   100%
                                 Acceptability'

The worst idea   *The best idea*
I've ever heard.   *I've ever heard.*

How do you get from point **A** to point **B**? This process is called 'Building' - making modifications to the original idea, adding features, exploring expanded applications. After the idea is inspired, we have to give it space and allow it to sprout. Then we have to nurture it until it blooms.

'Building' - when interacting with someone around their new idea, sounds like this ...

> "Your idea made me think that we could also ..."
> "Good point, and we could use that to ..."
> "That idea triggered a thought for me. What if we ..."

Δ   Try to use building lead-ins while working in meetings and on projects over the next few weeks. What differences do you see in the quality of the interactions? Key contributors know that for organizations to be successful and innovative, employees must respond to each other's ideas and initiatives in ways that find the value, encourage, and build shared commitment. Contributors practice this way of thinking in evaluating their own ideas, and they model this version of feedback in their interactions with others.

Ingenuity in Defining the Problem

Instant and early conclusions, solutions, suggestions, and statements about "how we solved that in the past" are the enemies of good problem solving. The good is, most often, the enemy of the better. Defining the problem and taking action occur almost simultaneously for most people. The mentally agile contributor paradoxically puts more energy into playing with the problem mentally - defining more creatively. Voluminous research on problem solving shows conclusively that the more effort one puts into the front end of the problem-solving process, the easier it is to come up with a good solution. This doesn't mean being inactive. It means being highly cognitively active in defining the problem more rigorously.

Δ   Define what the problem is and isn't. Providing solutions seems easy for everyone, so it would make sense to be sure that we are providing solutions to the right problems. Spend some time discussing the problem with colleagues. Separate out the elements that define the problem from those elements that seem to have nothing to do with the problem. Get a clear bead on a 'refined' problem definition.

Δ   Keep asking *"Why"?* See how many causes you can come up with and how many organizing buckets you can come up with. This exercise increases the chance of a better solution because you can see more connections.

Δ   Look for patterns in data; don't just collect information. The difference between data (facts) and *'information'* is that information consists of facts that have been organized and interpreted. Add some meaning to the data. Put them in context. Play with them in another frame. "Would these data mean the same thing if we had gathered it six years ago? ... five years from now"? "Does it mean the same thing in Switzerland as it does in our market in the United States"?

121

Quite often the context changes the 'meaning' quite dramatically.

Δ   Discipline yourself to pause for enough time to define the problem more completely. Always think of at least three solutions before you pick one. Some people have solutions in search of problems. They have favorite solutions. They have biases. They have universal solutions to most situations. They prejudge what the problem is without considering the nuances of this specific problem.

Δ   Look to see if you stated as facts things that are really assumptions or opinions. Did you generalize from a single example?

Δ   Don't jump to a solution. In studies of problem-solving sessions, solutions outweigh questions eight to one. Most meetings on a problem start with people offering a solution. Resist this impulse.

Δ   Set aside at least 50% of your time for questions and problem definition. Ask some more questions... even more than you think are necessary. Asking more questions early helps you rethink the problem and come up with more and different solutions.

Δ   Turn the problem upside down. Ask what is the least likely thing it could be. What the problem is not. What's missing from the problem, or what the mirror image of the problem might be. Here's a quick example of how this strategy works.

> *The Problem:* Imagine a single elimination tennis match with 127 players. How many matches total does it take to determine a winner? Well, the logical thinker might reason: there are 126 people paired off in 63 matches, plus one unpaired player in a bye. In the next round there are 64 players - matching all the previous winners and the player who drew a bye in the first round - in 32 matches. Most logical thinkers begin to create a mental tournament chart: first, 63

matches, then 32 subsequent matches, then 16, and so on. Add the number of matches from each round, and within a minute or so you have the answer. Those who are more mentally agile look at the problem differently and get the answer instantaneously. Forget about the winners. If you have 127 players, in order to come up with one champion, there must be 126 losers. To generate 126 losers, you need 126 matches. Problem solved.[49]

Nurture a Healthy Paranoia

There also seems to be a certain healthy paranoia in the mentally agile. They seem to say, "OK, we're doing well today, but we might not be doing well tomorrow, so we'd better be better at what we're doing today, and we'd better destroy our old established model before somebody else does it for us".

The *GAP's* former CEO Millard Drexler told his people that they should think about their comparable store performance as 'negative 15%'. Instead of celebrating the very positive numbers they had because of their dramatic growth, he advised his people to 'Act as though it were a negative 15%, and what are you going to do to bring it back'? [50]

This 'frame' creates a restless search for new ways to produce and a restless dissatisfaction with the current output.

Δ   No matter how well you're doing, act as if you could do better - and believe this to be the case. This creates an obsession with unmet opportunities, with new needs and new desires. It's very entrepreneurial. It empowers you to be as creative as possible and to spend some time challenging established models. It's that combination, the willingness to experiment and the will to always do better, that triggers the ability to change. It's what has organization contributors constantly improving what they are doing.

Chapter Three

Action Learning: The How-To's of Information Mining

"Learning organizations may be a tool not just for the evolution of organizations, but for the evolution of intelligence".
- Peter M. Senge

The High-Impact Participant-Observer

The various branches of military service are undoubtedly the experts at teaching survival skills in the ultimate of adverse conditions. New recruits and seasoned veterans alike learn how to survive using the acronym S.T.O.P. : **S**top, **T**hink, **O**bserve, **P**lan. There is no better description of the skillset of action learning. The careful reader will perhaps note that this advice seems to counter some of the aspects of mental agility - for example, quickness in thought and action and a well-calibrated intuitive skill. In the case of action learning, however, the skillset involves drawing important learning from ongoing organizational processes. Learning in this way represents a different kind of skill - a skill that involves a more considered taking-stock of what is actually occurring and how. Certainly in tough times, but even in the best of times, the ability to assist your organization in learning from its own processes and its own experiences will catapult you to the status of major player in the organization's success.

The individual with the skill of action learning is one who can be fully present and a high-impact contributor in every aspect of his or her work - offering input and bringing needed skills to the table. Equally important, however, is the ability to take a figurative step back from time to time to see the bigger picture and to draw learning from the process. The action learner is a *'cultural anthropologist'* of sorts, using a specific set of skills to gather important information, to assist in bringing meaning to that information, and to help organization members to learn from that information in order to work more effectively.

This skill is one of being able to think in 'systems' terms. Every once in a while, it is important to get off the merry-go-round and ask these questions:

- What are we doing?
- What should we be doing?
- What should we be doing next?
- What should we *not* be doing?

As organizations get leaner, it is important to find people at every level to lead. And leadership often involves asking the tough questions that organizations need to address. Leaders know how to facilitate and to expedite. This is the person who knows what to expect and how to work through it. Twenty-first-century organizations need leaders at all organization levels and individuals who can facilitate the work of others in the organization.

What Our Surveys Showed

When we analyzed the content of our surveys with key contributors and the managers who hired them, over 48% of those surveyed mentioned some aspect of what we have come to call *'Action Learning'*. Key individuals were known to display one or more of the following skills:

1. Observant Participation
2. Facilitating Collaborative Meaning
3. Leveraging Actionable Knowledge

Let's have a look at each of these skillsets in more detail.

1. Observant Participation

"We think too small. Like the frog at the bottom of the well. He thinks the sky is only as big as the top of the well. If he climbed to the surface, he would have an entirely different view".

- Based on a story in the *Chuang-Tsu*

'Inattentional Blindness': Two Studies

Professor Richard Wiseman of the *University of Herfordshire* in Great Britain performed the following fascinating study on a quality that has come to be called *inattentional blindness*.[51] The study consisted of giving subjects a newspaper and asking that they count the number of pictures in the paper. On page two, he inserted in huge inch-and-a-half letters:

"STOP COUNTING - THERE ARE 43 PHOTOGRAPHS IN THIS NEWSPAPER".

Many people missed this enormous headline. They were too busy counting photos. Those who saw the announcement right away were more likely to be individuals who were open to the surplus information around them and were able to take action in a slightly different way that more successfully accomplished the task.

Another message occurred further along in the paper:

"STOP COUNTING. TELL THE EXPERIMENTER YOU HAVE SEEN THIS AND WIN $250".

Again, the individuals who were able to stay alert to other possibilities spotted the opportunity and claimed the prize. Even though they were doing a specific job, they were open to additional information and other possibilities. This is one of the reasons why the same people - the contributors - keep making the breakthroughs. It's not a matter of luck - at least not in the way we normally define luck. 'Being in the right place at the right time' is more about being in the right frame of mind: more open and receptive to unexpected possibilities; more relaxed, with a heightened awareness of the world around them. These individuals spot and seize opportunities other people miss.

Daniel Simons and Christopher Chabris, two *Harvard University* psychologists, conducted a remarkable study in the elevator lobby of the fifteenth floor of the *Harvard* psychology department.[52] In the study, two teams of players (white shirts and black shirts) passed a basketball back and forth.. Experimental subjects were asked to watch a video of this activity and count the number of passes made by players dressed in white. In one video, a person dressed in a gorilla suit clearly walks through the middle of the scene for a period of about five seconds. Fifty-six percent of the subjects didn't even notice. In another video, the gorilla stops, faces the camera, pounds her chest, and then marches off. The gorilla was visible for nine seconds, yet only 50% of the subjects spotted it. Those who missed the ape tended to be individuals who were anxious, tense, sensitive to stress, and closed off. They were very serious and intense about their assignment and failed to pay attention to other things that were going on around them. Those who noticed were more laid-back and open to life's possibilities. If you can miss a gorilla in your midst, you're likely to miss the opportunities swirling all around you during the course of a busy business day or the course of a career.

This notion about 'observation' also connects in an interesting way with chance or luck People often quote Louis Pasteur - *'Chance favors the prepared mind'*. The whole quote has a slightly different connotation. *'Where observation is concerned, chance favors only the prepared mind.'* If you're not observing well, observing closely to begin with, no amount of preparation is enough.

It is often shocking how little of our environment we consciously perceive, especially if we're focused on a specific task. Once you've gained this insight, you can start opening yourself up to the possibilities (and important information) you may have been missing.

This skill - being in the frame of mind for observant participation - allows you to bring new information to the organization by virtue of observing the behavior of the system and its subsets and developing a deep understanding of the workings of the organization, taking a figurative step back from time to time to see the bigger picture... exactly like an anthropologist might understand another culture.

In psychological terms, this is called *'reframing'* - seeing the world from another frame of reference - which often provides a unique insight or a clearer understanding. Organizations typically have their own vernacular that speaks to the dangers of ignoring this observant-participation skill: "We're lost in the data", "We're down in the weeds", "We don't have the 35,000-foot view".

The ability to adopt the participant-observer role becomes especially useful when operating within a team environment - either as team leader or team member. Fully participating allows you to contribute to the team's effort while immersing yourself in the common experience. At the same time, being able to 'observe' the team's work often leads to a clearer understanding of the team's level of development and those actions needed to facilitate the team's work and forward movement.

The following quotes about key contributors are typical and are drawn directly from our surveys:

> "He has been very successful at helping his team move past roadblocks and take effective action based on the results and feedback they are gathering".

> "She has a very clear understanding of how a team develops and works most effectively".

> "He has real 'processing skills' - knowing not only what is being done, but how that work is accomplished most effectively".

> "He provides clear direction by making sure that every member of the work group has a good understanding of the task to be undertaken and the goals to be met".

2. Facilitating Collaborative Meaning

"The job of a leader isn't just to make decisions, it's to make sense".
-    John Seely Brown

Conversations as the New Work Style

Alan Webber, former editor of *Harvard Business Review* and cofounder of *Fast Company* magazine, in writing about the new economy stated:

> "Conversation is the core process by which humans think and coordinate their actions. Collective learning ensues and the resultant collective intelligence co-creates business and social value". [53]

Information alone is not *communication*. How does information become the kind of communication that moves an organization forward? Communication involves a *response* to the message. That's why live, in-person communication is so powerful. In person, you can sense immediately whether the other is responding to your message and in what way. In 'transactive talk' - to a live audience - there is power in human speech, and information multiplies. Hearing a CEO speak in a heartfelt manner about the organization's vision communicates much more, and at a deeper level, than a simple viewing of the PowerPoint slides. The organizational lesson here is that for organizations to truly mine the information that exists in the system, structured, multidirectional conversations, among those most directly involved, are essential.

The formula for maximizing information - and therefore knowledge and wisdom - in an organization is this:

"The right people …
           …having the right conversations …
                       …about the right things
                                   … at the right time". [54]

The key contributor with the skill of action learning recognizes that there is more to '*processing*' a group's or an organization's work. The 'more' is being able to bring *meaning* to the observed data. This involves a social action perspective - one in which personal bias is offset by including others in developing a '*shared understanding*' of what is taking place. Meaning is brought through collaborative discussion in which the patterns and their meanings are abstracted. High performance in the 21st century organization demands conversation. Conversations are the way we discover what we know. We share what we know with colleagues and, in the process, create new knowledge for the organization. We have coined the term '*co-operation*' to acknowledge the collaborative action of this way of working.

The following quotes about our contributors are typical and are drawn directly from our surveys:

> "He led meetings in such a way that things were talked through completely before any decisions were made. Potential actions were looked at from every angle, and ways were designed to overcome any potential obstacles".

> "She makes sure that everyone on the team is involved and participating in the planning process".

> "He levels with others on where he stands, and they seem to do the same with him. This makes solving problems much more effective".

> "He shows the ability to work with other people as equals, to respect what they bring to the table, to listen to them for ideas, and to work cooperatively with others to accomplish the task at hand".

> "He can walk the tightrope of adopting a low personal profile but facilitating the work of others well".

> "He has the ability to develop ideas by discussion with others".

3. Leveraging "Actionable Knowledge"

"I know not anything more pleasant, or more instructive, than to compare experience with expectation, or to register from time to time the difference between idea and reality. It is by this kind of observation that we grow daily less liable to be disappointed".

- Samuel Johnson

Learning by Doing

The most powerful sequence for leveraging the knowledge that an organization creates is:

Reflection.... on what has been done

Insight Harvesting ... capturing the lessons learned

Implementation ... taking the next step

Action Planning ... determining the next step

Feedback ... learning from our actions

Key contributors initiate action themselves, and they lead the informed actions of others. They gather *feedback* to capture the learning from their actions, use that feedback to *plan and implement* next steps, *harvest* new information from the results of those actions, and *reflect* on what has been discovered. This sequence allows an *integrating* of what has been learned and a *generalizing* of this learning to new situations. Contributors understand that information is data endowed with relevance and purpose. Converting data to information requires an understanding of how that data can be used to enhance action. Knowledge, derived from action, folded into organizational purpose and initiative, becomes valuable. Knowledge, in turn, becomes *wisdom* when it is used to anticipate future contingencies, to solve distantly related problems, and to be applied to other areas of organizational life not directly related to the area from which the initial knowledge was gathered. Truly knowledgeable people tend toward continuous learning, whatever their field, precisely because they understand that there is always so much more to know.

Survivors of every kind of adverse occurrence have relied on a skill military survival schools refer to as *'situational awareness'* - knowing what is going on around you *and* being able to act on that knowledge. High-performance companies (and individuals) focus not only on the *what* of the organization's work, but also on the *how* - how people and resources connect for accomplishment. After-action reviews provide important information that might otherwise go unnoticed in the hustle and bustle of the workday. Key contributors help their organizations by employing the insight and understanding of the *'sociological observer'* to observe and experience the world, retaining an observer's eye for analysis, reflection, and understanding. This skill involves digging beneath the surface and raising important 'cultural' issues that might otherwise be unspoken. Once this information has been surfaced, action is required. Based on what you know and what you have discovered, what can you *do* to use this knowledge to improve things?

After-action reviews stress four themes:

- Everyone needs to think about what they're learning all the time.
- Everyone needs to get clear on the big picture.
- Sometimes the most important information comes from examining the situation when things are going wrong.
- Fostering benevolent self-criticism and seeking to learn from the process is essential.

Such review and 'processing' helps to unfreeze old patterns of behavior and create openings for new understanding and new behaviors to take root. This is the candid give-and-take that is a necessary part of performance improvement.

The following quotes about key contributors are typical and are drawn directly from our surveys:

> "He has been very successful at helping his team move past roadblocks and take effective action".

"He is a good critical thinker and can be incisive in directing a team's efforts along productive lines".

"When she was part of the project team, she made sure that the team emphasized drawing conclusions and basing actions on observable data".

"She leads her group in a discussion of what's gone right and what's gone wrong before they implement any further action".

"He was the best in the department at teasing out what worked and what didn't, and helping us find a way to improve".

Active Stance   **Receptive Nature**

Initiative

Collaboration

Mental Agility

Action Learning

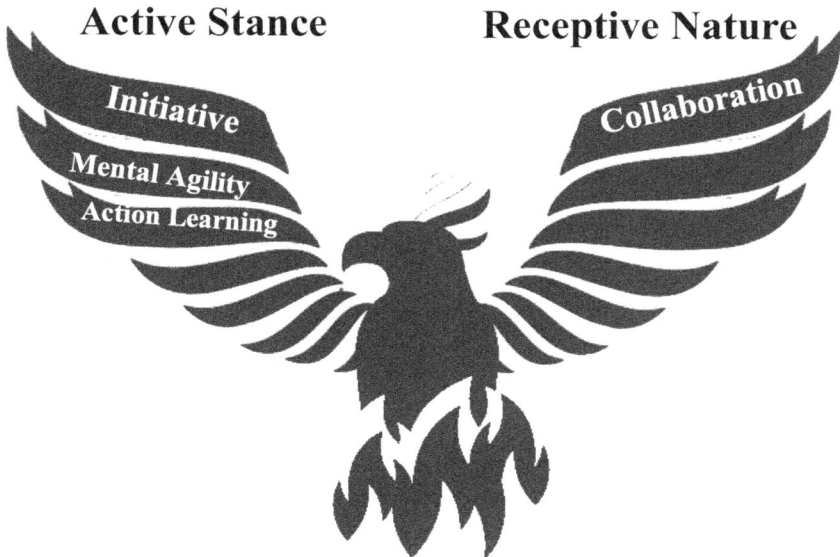

Are You An Action Learner?

It's time to test your knack for *'Action learning'*. Do you possess this key strategy? Take this short quiz and find out. For each set of descriptors, those on the right of the page and those on the left, check the ones that apply to you. Check as many items as are descriptive of your work style. Your task here is to make as honest an assessment of your skills as possible. The results will help you to understand how natural this ability is for you and, if you choose, guide you to activities and exercises in the next section of this chapter designed to develop the skill of 'action learning'.

☐	I think it's most important to meet our work objectives even if that means pushing ahead despite the objections of some of the group members.	☐	I tend to look at not only *what* my work group is doing, but *how* that work is accomplished most effectively.
☐	Monitoring the work group is the leader's responsibility.	☐	I can be pretty effective in appraising the work group's efforts and redirecting them along more productive lines when necessary
☐	Driving execution - getting the objective met - is what defines effectiveness.	☐	I believe that it is important to examine our processes to see what's working and what is not in order to move us past roadblocks.
☐	I am primarily interested in making sure our group's objectives are being met.	☐	I am considered to be insightful and perceptive in looking at the work style of my group.
☐	When we follow our work plan as it has been laid out, we can usually be very effective.	☐	I consider myself to be a troubleshooter - looking to meet the needs of the occasion and correcting problems as they arise.
☐	I sometimes become frustrated when the group is not working well together.	☐	I can usually see what is blocking my group's effective functioning and assist in moving past these roadblocks to effective action.
☐	The group leader should be the one to call attention to group problems when they occur.	☐	I am outspoken in addressing problems and can be convincing in helping the group to remedy the situation.
☐	I work best alone, where I can focus my energy without the interruption of others.	☐	I prefer working in a group of other competent people, rather than working independently.

☐	My group spends way too much time hashing over the issues before we make decisions.	☐	In meetings, I like to talk things out thoroughly before coming to a conclusion.
☐	The work group should be directed in its activity by the leader or the one designated to head up a particular action.	☐	I work to make sure that all work-group members feel included and valued as an important part of the team, so that they are able to participate fully.
☐	In a group setting, conflicts should be minimized, and we should move forward quickly.	☐	I believe that it is important to get all the important issues out in the open and work to resolve any differences that exist.
☐	The most knowledgeable and persuasive members should drive the group's action.	☐	I respect what everyone brings to the table. I try hard to reach for ideas and to work cooperatively with others to accomplish the task at hand.
☐	Often there is way too much discussion of a course of action. The group should make a decision based on the most persuasive argument and move forward quickly.	☐	When there is doubt about a course of action, the group should make sure that everyone's perspective has been considered. Open discussion is the best way to find the way forward.
☐	I believe we usually have the actions outlined well before we begin any task.	☐	I encourage the work group to evaluate the "pros and cons" of its chosen approach to the task or project.

☐	I believe that it is important to follow a project or action to its conclusion before making any decisions about its effectiveness.	☐ I encourage the work group to reevaluate and direct its efforts when it becomes clear that work goals are not being met.
☐	Outlining the tasks to be done should allow everyone to take their part in the project.	☐ It is important for the group to clarify roles and establish who is responsible for what before we begin any action or project.
☐	It is important to bring the project to completion before it can be thoroughly evaluated.	☐ We can learn from taking action if we measure our results and alter our course on the fly as necessary, based on the results we are getting.
☐	Once a task has been completed, it's important to move on quickly to the next project in order to keep our productivity high.	☐ Careful after-action review can generate new information to make our next efforts more effective
☐	The facts of any situation should speak for themselves and require no elaborate interpretation.	☐ It's important to make sense out of the data we generate by looking at the information in the context of the organization's purpose and environment.
☐	Organizational data should be fed up the organization in order for its relevance to be determined by those at the top.	☐ Having ongoing conversations with those most involved is necessary to make sense of the results the group or organization generates
- _____ **Total Boxes Checked**		+ _____ **Total Boxes Checked**

Our survey results indicate that over 48% of respondents mentioned some aspect of what we have come to call '*Action Learning*'. Recall that our respondents were either organization key contributors themselves or managers who had the task of selecting employees to advance their organization in a critical time. They occupied all levels of the organization, from executives to individual contributors. In every case, respondents were asked to comment on those skills that they believed made employees indispensable to their companies.

Add the numbers in the Totals boxes together, retaining their arithmetic sign. If your score is between -20 and -10, your action learning ability is underdeveloped. You may be hampered by a tendency to focus only on your task and not learn from your experience nor contribute to the organization more broadly - a significant handicap in an organizational culture where ongoing learning has become a desired outcome. Your action learning contributor skills would be increased by attending to and practicing the exercises and activities in the next section of this chapter.

If your total score is between +10 and +20, it is likely that your action learning skills are serving you well. Nevertheless, you may wish to review the exercises and activities in the next section of this chapter to assist you in further developing these skills.

Become A High-Impact Participant-Observer

The skillset of action learning is the ability to assist your organization and its members in learning from their own processes. Key contributors have this ability, to take a figurative step back from time to time to see the bigger picture and to draw learning from the process. They can get off the merry-go-round and ask the important questions: What are we doing? What *should* we be doing? What should we be doing next? What should we *not* be doing?

Those who have mastered the skillset of action learning are '*cultural anthropologists*' of sorts, using a specific set of skills to gather important information, to assist in bringing meaning to that information, and to help organization members to learn from that information in order to work more effectively. Contributors think in 'systems' terms.

This is a set of skills that is learnable by everyone. If you want to add to your capability in the area of action learning, here are some tips to help you sharpen this capacity.

As you read through the Skill Builders associated with each aspect of *Action Learning*, circle the symbol beside those you would like to implement. Then use Table 5 in the Appendix to fill out aspects of your '*Action Learning Kit*'.

1. Observant Participation

Organization contributors with the skillset of action learning are able to be fully present and participating, but are also able to take a figurative step back from time to time to see the bigger picture.

Skill Builders:

℧   Consider a *'closed mouth'* strategy [55] – at least initially. To repeat a famous quote from an anonymous source: *"I've often regretted my speech, but never my silence"*. The lucky among us realize that too much talk can lock us into positions that seem right today but may be wrong tomorrow. Guard against unnecessary talk. Listen for the lesson. Silence can give you the freedom to react flexibly to unexpected events.

Δ   As important as taking the time to observe is the wisdom of knowing where to look and what to look for. Carefully watch your organization or your team's work style. Take note of these things:
- What are the hot issues?
- What is the level of participation among members?
- How do we generate alternatives?
- How do we evaluate our progress?
- How is conflict handled when it surfaces?
- How about leadership?: Who is influencing whom?

- Roles: Who does what?
- Goals: What are we trying to accomplish?
- Norms: What are the ground rules? What actions are deemed appropriate? Which are inappropriate?
- Climate/tone: What's the feeling level in the group?
- What is communicated, both verbally and nonverbally? Nonverbal communication - body language, facial expressions, how people choose to arrange themselves in a room for a group session, customary and accepted ways of greeting one another - all contribute to your accurately and completely documenting the true-lived experience: the '*culture*' of the organization.
- Which initiatives tend to get worked... and which are left off?
- How organization members arrange themselves in space and time for meetings provides important clues about the culture, including the operating style and human interaction that is allowed and endorsed.
    - Do participants at meetings arrange themselves around a conference table, or do most sit in chairs against the wall?
    - How are speaking times allotted? Does one person direct the questions and respondents orient towards him or her, or do participants address one another?
    - Do participants regularly arrive late to meetings? Do they carry on other business: checking their notebooks, cell phones, reading?

These 'activity traces' reveal valuable information about underlying patterns of behavior and choices that the organization makes to accomplish its work, and answer the question: "What (if anything) needs to be changed about the way we are working"? When you develop an awareness of these organizational cultural issues, you have captured the knowledge to help your organization work more effectively.

Δ   Pay attention to organization documents. They offer valuable information about what the organization values, where it places its major emphasis (at least for public consumption), and what is supposedly rewarded. Have a look at the policy manuals, training materials, minutes of meetings, memoranda, computerized data files. These are particularly valuable in comparing whether programs and policies in the field are indeed being carried out and working as intended.

Δ   Observe what does *not* happen: Often what does not happen is as important to understand as what does happen.

        Let's say a meeting is intended to be 'highly participative in nature', at least according to the training manuals, but you observe some of these sessions in action and you consistently notice that the members do not speak up, do not volunteer their own experiences, and do not share their own stories. Rather, you notice that the 'leader' seems to be sort of 'top-down' controlling the conversation - doing most of the talking in the form of directives and suggestions. Noticing and recording that an intended event (members freely initiating conversation) did *not* happen may be a gold-mine discovery about an organization's true culture. This discovery and mismatch, in turn, can spur further investigation as to why such intended outcomes are not occurring. The answers to those questions can help propel an organization forward.

Δ   Dig into surprises: Suppose that an activity or work session is planned, and it either does not take place or something goes wrong with the execution. The observant participant watches with intense interest to see how everyone reacts to this. Do they get angry? Disappointed? Frustrated? And then, what do they decide to do? You may observe that after an initial 'ain't it awful' gripe session, someone pipes up with, *'Say, let's take some time right after work to talk about these issues. I know a room where we can meet for a few minutes and at least get our ideas out'.* And then another person chimes in, *'OK, that's a great idea'!* Before you know

142

it, they've divided up who will bring the flip charts, who will set up the room and where, how long they will meet. Lost opportunity? Hardly! We've learned a great deal about the culture of the organization in regard to 'team building', 'decision making', and 'cooperation'. Such is the beauty of many such golden opportunities to observe and learn.

Δ   Look at informal interactions and unplanned activities - these are often the richest and most revealing slices of life in terms of diagnosing the culture of the organization. For example, consider how members spend their free / unstructured time. If you are attending a planned activity, such as a conference or all-hands meeting, what do participants choose to do during their free time? With whom do they gather? These are wonderful opportunities to observe the organization culture in action. The fact that none of the participants talk about a session when it is over is data. The fact that people immediately split in different directions when a session is over is data. The fact that people talk about personal interests and share gossip that has nothing to do with the program is data.

Δ   Try your hand at '*definitional mapping*'. This is a technique related to observant participation. The labels that people use - those that affect them and become incorporated into the lingo - are often illuminating indicators of the nature of the organization. What are your organization's 'buzzwords' and how are they used? What impact do they have on employee activity? Consider the following:

- "Paradigm shift"
- "At the end of the day …"
- "35,000-foot view"
- "Down in the weeds"
- "Learning organization"

☼   You will increase your value to your organization if you make it a habit to create a '*mental debrief*' (or a more formal work diary) of what happens at every organizational watershed moment:

143

- What happens at important meetings… headlines of the content, but more detailed notes about the interactions and the 'unspoken' details - feeling tone, levels of participation, and enthusiasm. What seemed to work to get everybody onboard and what fell flat?
- Who among your colleagues are proving to be your most important contacts? Not your 'friends', but who is it most important for you to know and to keep a solid relationship with? Why are they so important?
- What are the significant events that take place? Do they line up with a specific organizational function? Are the same people always involved in these important events? What do the events signal? How can you become a more central part of the action?

Δ   Be aware that there is considerable advantage to being able to process a group's work 'online'- as opposed to waiting until the end of the project, as is more commonly done. If things are going well, processing can validate what is being done well and can guide you to the next level of development. If things are not going well, processing can help you to learn what *is* going on. It may sensitize you to some 'unfinished business' - often indicative of some issues left unresolved, underlying conflicts, or the possibility of 'groupthink'.

☼   Be able to distinguish between activities that keep you 'down in the weeds' from those that give you the bigger picture – 'the 35,000-foot view'. A lofty vantage point allows you to see your organization in action much more clearly.

2. Facilitating Collaborative Meaning

Key contributors know that there is more to 'processing' a group's or an organization's work. The 'more' is being able to bring meaning to the observed data. This involves a social action perspective - one in which personal bias is offset by including others in developing a 'shared understanding' of what is taking place. Meaning is brought through collaborative discussion where the patterns and their meanings are understood. People who don't have time to think about what they are going to do next, much less talk about it, become extremely myopic and overly task-focused. Their stance often becomes one of "What's the least amount of work I can do to get this done"? Building in a process to talk through the issues and bring collaborative meaning to the project not only broadens your perspective, but greatly improves the quality of the work.

Conversations are inspiring. Amazing ideas have come from simple, innocent conversations. Conversations have led to ideas for new products, novels, new businesses, strategic plans, and even business books! Having someone else to bounce ideas off of, to push against, or to argue with, is often the turning point for a great idea. Even after an idea is inspired, you have to give it space and allow it to sprout.

Skill Builders:

Δ   Level with people on where you stand on the issues, and invite them to do the same with you.

Δ   Take a closer look at how things get done in your organization. Ask some key questions:
- What are our core values and competencies?
- How do these values and competencies get displayed or acted upon?
- What's more valued: short-term goals or long-term objectives?
- How are decisions made around here?
- How much risk is tolerated? What kinds of risks are acceptable?
- What other data exist about how this organization operates?

Once you have the answers to some of these questions, feed them back to others and get their reactions and reflections. Better still, explore these questions together.

Δ   Offer what you have observed during the team meetings (when appropriate). Ask for reactions from others. Meaning is brought to activity through collaborative discussion. Encourage talking things out before coming to conclusions

145

or a decision.

Δ   Involving others in finding the way brings broader perspective to the discussion as the group seeks to make sense of the data. Such collaborative discussion helps to minimize personal bias and can cut to the core of the issues of importance.

Δ   Bring in others to consult with you (even for a few minutes in quick hallway consults). Review what you've done or what you plan to do and see if they have any suggestions or advice. It could save you a huge amount of time if you're headed in a wrong direction and will greatly enhance your results.

Δ   The first step toward understanding and shared meaning is the skill of empathy. Instead of telling people what they ought to do or becoming tyrannically optimistic, inquire about others' ideas and feelings. Cultivating empathy has its own rewards - the more you do it, the better your relationships, the more you want to involve others, and the more complete is your understanding of the issues. Empathy is life's connective tissue.

3. Leveraging "Actionable Knowledge"

Key contributors make use of a specific step-by-step process to make organizational knowledge '*actionable*'. The reflection / insight-harvesting / action-planning / implementation / feedback sequence can multiply organizational learning. Key contributors initiate action themselves and lead the informed actions of others. They harvest new information from the results of those actions. This allows an *integrating* of what has been learned and a *generalizing* of this learning to new situations.

Skill Builders:

Δ   Make use of what has been called "*PMI thinking.*" For any proposed course of action, or any idea for that matter, examine it more carefully by asking (and answering) three

specific questions:
- What are the '**P**lusses' of this course of action?
- What are the '**M**inuses' (or drawbacks) of this course of action?
- What's '**I**nteresting' about this course of action?

Once you have examined your course of action in this way, in all likelihood you have uncovered lots of useful information that might better guide you along your path or change your path all together.

Δ   While looking at the pros and cons of every situation, stay aware of the '*Law of Unintended Consequences*' - those potentially adverse outcomes that are not part of the plan but often surface if careful foresight has not anticipated them. Ask "What might be some things that could result if we do this, even though that's not what we intend to happen"?

Δ   In each after-action review, harvest the new information from the results. Use this information to plan further action, refine your efforts or approach, carefully integrate what you have learned, and decide how you might generalize this learning to new or different situations.

Change "Traps" or Transformational Change?

The business landscape is not the same as it was even a few decades ago. The organizational environment has become increasingly turbulent. The pace of technological innovation, company mergers, acquisitions, bankruptcies, downsizing, globalization of markets, increasing consumer influence, and changes in the law has intensified the need for change. But how organizations change also seems to have shifted. In the 1950's and 1960's, change in organizations was primarily incremental. People adapted and were rewarded for their new behavior. During the 1960's and 1970's, change became more rapid. Individuals responded by working smarter not harder. The 1980's and 1990's and the movement into the 21st century brought even more rapid and unpredictable change. In any case, today the message to American business is clear: *change or disappear.*

The changes organizations make differ in size, scope, and impact. Organizational development specialists have come to look at organizational change as consisting of two varieties: *'first-order change'* and *'second-order change'*.

First-Order Change

This type of change is referred to as *'deviation-correcting'* change. It is adaptive and incremental, is continuous in nature, and involves no major shifts in how the organization operates. It involves only modifications, adjustments, and adaptations to already existing processes and procedures. The nature of the organization and its tasks stay relatively the same. This type of change is aimed at improved functioning within the organization – 'doing things better'. Changes are minor and 'evolutionary' in nature. They typically involve transitions and fine-tuning. It is step-by-step movement along a well-worn path, representing variations in degree within an existing framework, based on precedent. The aim is to do 'more of the same, only better'.

First-order change is most appropriate when the present system is essentially adequate to support the current objectives. The system and its environment appear stable, and no dramatic change in conditions (technology, competition, or regulation) has occurred.

In addition, first-order change seems the likely choice when there exists a backlog of incremental change possibilities whose benefits outweigh their costs. First-order change methods direct efforts toward minor modifications in organizational structures, job redesign, management practices, policies and procedures, team building (helping teams to function more effectively), intergroup problem solving, and process consulting.

An example of first-order change is continuously improving the efficiency of production in an assembly or manufacturing operation. Tuning up a car so that it runs more smoothly captures the nature of this type of change. First-order change looks like this… making minor adjustments to keep things 'on track'.

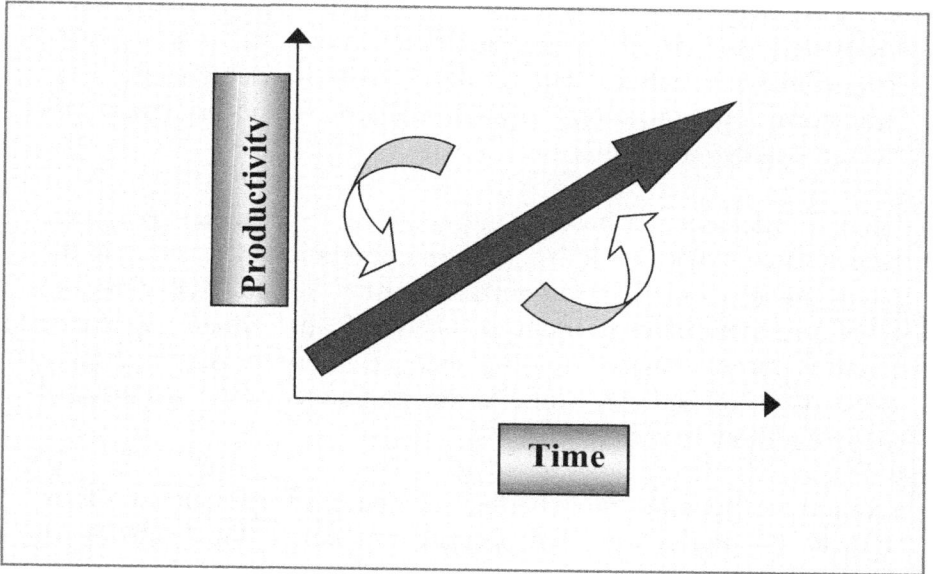

Δ   Does your organization need only first-order change strategies?

- Is the organization basically in tune with the market environment?
- Does the organization simply need to do more of something, do less of something, tweak the processes, or simply get back on track? If so, first-order change methods are probably all that are required.

Second-Order Change

Often referred to as '*discontinuous*' change, second-order change is system-wide and 'game-changing' in nature. It is transformational for an organization. Such change requires significant changes in the organization and its tasks. Second-order change affects the fundamental character of the system. Often a series of incremental changes have been implemented that have resulted in gradually diminishing returns. Eventually a crisis will arise, and transformational change will become necessary for the organization to survive. Many different levels of the organization and many different aspects of the business are involved in change of this type.

149

Interventions directed toward the organization's mission, strategy, leadership, and culture will result in second-order change. This 'transforms' organizations through changes in the organization's overall strategy and culture.

Second-order change became more critical as organizations were forced to cope with rapid, radical, and unpredictable change in the environment or market. Organizations often found it necessary to transform themselves in order to survive. Transformational change requires more demands on top leaders - more visioning, more experimenting, and more time in the simultaneous management of many additional variables.

Examples of second-order changes include: shifting operations from a focus on production of a specific product to the licensing of production processes and technologies, or a restaurant changing its concept from neighborhood deli to upscale haute cuisine.

Second-order change often includes interventions such as: organizational visioning and future search, organizational culture change, a focus on how organizations learn, '*total quality management*' *(TQM)* approaches, reengineering of processes, major changes in technology, changes in organizational structure, and changes in the nature of the organization's relationships with the employees and customers. Second-order change looks like this... a major shift that changes the way the organization does business, not just getting back on track.

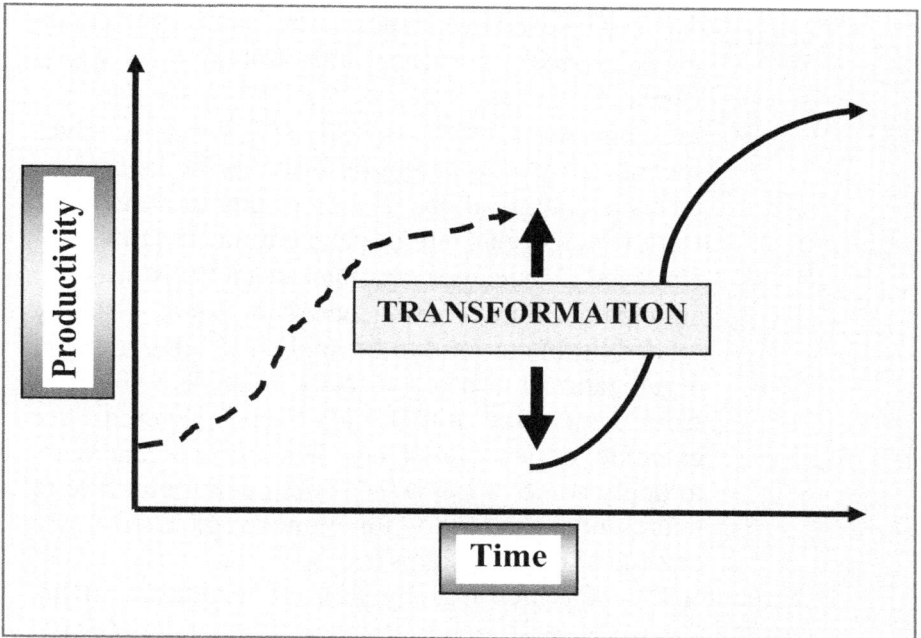

△ Does your organization require second-order change?
- Have there been fundamental shifts in the market that make the organization less viable?
- Have policies and regulations changed in such a way that some transformation of the organization's processes is required?
- Has there been a new niche discovered that would change the look and feel of the organization?

△ Take the lead and assist others in making the translation from data to organizational meaning.
- The fact is that data by themselves are meaningless. The thought that the most important thing is the detail is not always correct. Sometimes the most important thing is the 'big picture' - and the discernment to know when each detail is most important.
- Data becomes *information* when it is endowed with relevance and purpose. Converting data into information requires an understanding of how that

151

data can be used to enhance action. Facts, folded into organizational purpose and initiative, become valuable.

- Moving from information to *knowledge* involves specialization. Expanding information in its various forms and applications creates a body of knowledge from which organizations can continue to draw.
- Knowledge becomes *wisdom* when it is used to anticipate future contingencies, to solve distantly related problems, and to be applied to other areas of organizational life not directly related to the area from which the initial data were gathered. For example, organizations have learned in recent years to apply some of the laws of the natural universe to help understand the functioning of their own complex human systems.

Structure your activities in such a way as to capitalize on this formula, and you will greatly increase your organization's learning.

Δ   Ask yourself and lead the discussion with others around the following questions:

- Who are the 'right people' for this project?
- What kind of conversations would move us forward?
- What are the things that we most need to talk about?
- What is irrelevant or distracting?
- When is the right time to move on this?

As you help your organization to structure conversations in this way, you will multiply your organization's ability to learn and earn for yourself a prominent place in the process.

Chapter Four

Visibility: Making Your Competence Unmistakable

"If you done it, it ain't bragging".
- Dizzy Dean

"It's a low dog who won't wag his own tail".
- Anonymous

Imagine this: A producer from the local *News at 6* television program is looking for rank-and-file business people (not CEOs) to come onto the show and talk about the future of American business from the standpoint of those in various industries. Or perhaps a writer from your local newspaper is doing a story on average people who have made a key difference in the businesses they work for. Would *you* get the call to be on the show or to be interviewed? Consider that for every worthwhile business endeavor, there are legions of other qualified people with the same set of credentials as yours. How will you distinguish yourself? What will you say, what will you do to ensure that you stand out, are recognized, and ultimately take the top prize? What seeds have you planted for your success? The ability and willingness to master the combination of things that lead to such visible competence can set you apart from others. Whether you are a job beginner or an established executive, you can stand out from the crowd - if you know how.

Flying under the radar may be an effective short-term survival strategy. But if you've only successfully flown under the radar during your career, when real opportunities come your way, you've left no impression at all - not a bad impression (which is probably what you wanted to avoid), but you haven't left a good impression either. If your colleagues don't know you and don't know about your competence, you're still out in the cold!

Make Yourself the Guru in Your Organization

In decades past a person could labor in obscurity and still have job security. Not any longer. Look at yourself from the company's point of view. In the good old days, the company elders may have considered your long years of service, your loyalty through the organization's good and bad times, your steadiness and dependability, and even your financial obligations. No more! Now you've got to make the case that your experience is worth something, that you have actually learned some lessons through all those years in the trenches that make you a valuable commodity. And the way you do that is by making sure the people who count recognize your value - that the people in the know, know you. You've got to find a way to let the folks on top know exactly how you contribute to the enterprise. Slogging along and turning in a solid performance is no longer good enough. You've got to be seen as a standout. You have to be someone strong enough to take on the 'impossible' jobs. You've got to show that you can step in and deliver immediately. No company is looking for bench strength right now. Your value is a product and needs to be packaged accordingly.

A Cohort of Competition

In an era of unpredictability, being recognized as a distinguished contributor isn't just a good idea - it's a necessity. In the short run, of course, you can be the unfortunate victim of a bad economy, a dying organization, a toxic boss, or a global pandemic. But in the long run, over the course of a career, there are simply no excuses. You and you alone are in control of your career. You are the one responsible for making your work life as productive and successful as it can be.

In the last 40 years, organizations have changed their architecture. There has been a transformation from silo-shaped organizations in which everyone stayed within their narrow job functions, to organizations that are now more horizontally-structured, team-based, and interdependent. Try to go it alone or hide in the wings in these organizations, and you'll be out in the cold, in favor of the one who is better known and better connected. Lean organizations dictate a new reality - that leaders must be found at every level. Looking up the organization for leadership just doesn't work anymore. Business is changing too rapidly. Top executives must be able to clearly identify and make use of *all* the talent that exists in the organization, or face the consequences in the worldwide marketplace. Build a name for yourself as a problem-solver, and you'll be a valuable person to have around. Organizations depend on people who can take care of problems, not just point them out. Come to the table with a thought-out solution to a critical or persistent organization problem, and you will be both visible *and* indispensable. Achieving visibility depends on several factors. Technical competence can get you to the starting gate. But creating a reputation as someone who is critical to the organization's success is what puts you in the lead.

Oh, Gosh, It Was Nothing ... Really

Working to achieve visibility is a difficult concept for many of us. We associate the prospect with braggadocio, arrogance, or blatant self-promotion. The fact is, the inability to make your competence *visible* in your organization means your career is suffering. Hesitance to make your contribution known in the organization derails otherwise promising careers, short-circuits potential, and delays or prevents promotions and pay raises. Invisible competence is of no use to anybody - not to you as an individual and certainly not to your company. Your competence must be visible to those in the organization who are able to reward your efforts and to those on whom your work depends. When you hesitate to make your hard work and your contribution known, you create a competency vacuum. As you can probably validate from your own experience, often someone less competent will come forward to fill that void. You also know, from your own experience, that those who succeed are not always the most loyal, the most talented, nor the most knowledgeable individuals within the organization. *But* they do have one very tangible asset: *They are widely recognized as having the skills that the organization values.*

Many of us labor under a self-limiting myth that contributes to our 'invisibility' - the *'myth of craftsmanship'*, the idea that 'good work speaks for itself'. Organization contributors know that, in fact, good work speaks for itself only if you give it a voice. Recent years have seen the rise of what has been called the 'entrepreneurial economy': 'championing' a product, an idea, or a career, and giving it a powerful voice. In *any* contact-dependent endeavor, success requires *both* effective performance *and* effective self-promotion - making your competence and your ability to contribute *visible*. If you can't do that, you will be passed over for promotion during succession planning time, or when the company is determining the best performers (and which individuals to keep) during tough economic times. Even if you're an ace at keeping your boss up to speed, remember that in today's fluid business climate, he or she might be gone tomorrow. You need to cover all your bases and stand out in the eyes of your boss's boss and that boss's boss and all the bosses up to the big boss.

What Makes Your "Product" Stand Out from the Crowd?

A wealth of research studies has examined what combination of activities leads to individual success in interdependent organizations.[49] Although results vary somewhat from study to study, the findings tend to group around the following mix of activities and their relative contribution to overall success:

- Focused work on the technical aspects of the job -10%
- Having a positive image within the organization - 30%
- Having an extensive network of personal contacts - 60%

John Kotter, Professor of Leadership at *Harvard Business School*, has studied a number of successful 'leaders' in major U.S. corporations, examining what their jobs entail and how they behave during a typical workday. These individuals were not necessarily the designated leaders in the organization, but rather were those who were universally recognized as being primarily responsible for the effective functioning and overall success of the endeavor. He observed their daily routines, interviewed key colleagues, and measured their performance. Several interesting findings emerged.[56]

- They spend most of their time with others. The average highly productive person spends only about 25% of his or her working time alone. Few spend less than 70% of their time with others, and some spend up to 90% of their work time working with colleagues.
- They spend time with many people in addition to their direct subordinates, their colleagues, and their bosses. They regularly interact with people who may appear to be unimportant to outsiders.
- The breadth of topics in their discussions is extremely wide. They do not limit the focus of their conversations to planning business strategy, project steps, cost concerns, or problem solving, strictly speaking. They discuss virtually anything and everything even remotely associated with their business.
- They ask a lot of questions. In a half-hour conversation, some would ask literally hundreds of questions.
- They often attempt to influence others. Instead of telling people what to do, however, they ask, request, cajole, persuade, and in various ways exert their considerable influence.

What Our Surveys Showed

When we analyzed the content of our surveys of key contributors and the managers who hired them, over 68% of those surveyed mentioned at least one of the aspects of what we have come to call *'Visibility'*. Those individuals, well-known in their organizations as contributors, are known for displaying one or more of these skills that contribute to their reputation. Five distinct aspects emerged that together make up visibility:

1. Being Widely Known in the Organization
2. Being Known as Competent
3. Being a Clear Communicator of Ideas
4. Being the Center of a Knowledge Network
5. Continuous Résumé-ing

Let's have a look at each of these aspects of visibility in more detail.

1. Being Widely Known in the Organization

"Nobody ever got a promotion by quietly going about their business, laboring in obscurity".

- Tom Peters

Consider the Spider

Max Gunther,[57] a journalist with a fascination for "luck" and theories about "luck," collected the stories of hundreds of people who were widely recognized as either spectacularly lucky or disastrously unlucky. He also interviewed psychiatrists, gamblers, Wall Street investors, scientists, and many others with an interest in the workings of luck. He discovered that the very lucky *are* different. In fact, they share several traits and patterns of behavior conspicuously absent in the unlucky. The lucky among us seem to know these by instinct. But they are skills that the rest of us can acquire. One such *'luck adjustment'* Gunther refers to as the *'Spiderweb Structure'*:

> The spider strings many lines to catch passing flies. The bigger her web, the better she eats. So it is with those who would catch good luck. In general, lucky men and women have taken the trouble to form a great many friendly contacts with other people.

Gunther gives us a practical example. Consider a corporate headhunter. The candidates he finds and eventually presents to his client are all people who have, in one way or another, made themselves *visible.* How did they do it?

- Some have done so deliberately... they joined and networked.
- The majority never gave much thought to being tapped. Most are simply people who have made themselves known to many other people... usually without thinking about it. It's their style. They're gregarious. They go out of their way to be friendly. They talk to strangers. They're joiners - meeters and greeters. If they sit next to somebody on a plane, they start a conversation. When good fortune - the right job, the

158

> right opportunity, the high-profile project, or the chance for promotion presents itself, *this is the kind of person who can be found.*
>
> The bigger your web of friendly contacts, the better the odds in your favor.

At the most basic level, one becomes visible in an organization because he or she is social - is *known by others.*

People who are 'visible' are intensely social people. They know everyone and everyone knows them. They are the ones everybody talks to the most: the 'go-to person', who, if they don't have the answer themselves, they know where to direct you so that you can get the information you need. (However, they will most likely go there and get it for you.)

Their circle of acquaintances is four to five times the size of most of ours. But it's more than just 'networking' or handing out your business card at meetings of strangers. These are people with a truly extraordinary knack for making friends and acquaintances. It's not a strategy, and they aren't aggressive about it. They're not backslappers, for whom the process of acquiring acquaintances is obvious and self-serving. It simply seems to be a natural gift for making social connections. They like people and find the patterns of acquaintanceship and interaction to be endlessly fascinating. They collect people the way others collect art or antiques. For most of us, the purpose of making an acquaintance is to evaluate whether we want to turn that person into a friend. Most of us don't feel we have the time or energy to maintain meaningful contact with everyone. Those who acquire visibility are different. They don't shy away from the obligation that might be required to maintain connections with someone they might run into only once or twice a year.[58]

The following quotes about these key contributors are typical and are drawn directly from our surveys:

> "She developed the people who worked under her and sent dozens of effective people out into the organization. She has allies everywhere".

159

"He has an extremely wide network of friends and acquaintances who hold him in very high regard. He has access to lots of people who have the capacity to help him when he needs it".

"The people that work for and with him know that they can go to him for anything".

"He is extremely likable and can do and say the correct thing in social situations with a quality that other people admire".

"She has the ability to make a strong and positive impact on the majority of people she meets".

Masters of the Weak Tie

Organization key contributors have mastered what sociologists call the *'weak tie'*: a friendly yet casual social connection. Sociologist Mark Granovetter [59] found that 56% of people he talked to found their jobs through a personal connection. Nothing surprising here. But of those personal connections, most were described as 'weak ties': people who were seen 'only occasionally' or 'rarely'. When it comes to finding new jobs, new information, or new ideas of any sort, weak ties are always more important than strong ties. Your friends, after all, occupy the same world that you do. Your acquaintances, by definition, occupy a much different world and are more likely to know something you don't. To capture this paradox, Granovetter coined the wonderful term *'the strength of the weak tie'*. Acquaintances represent a source of 'social power', expanding your reputation into areas where you might not otherwise be known. The more acquaintances you have, the more powerful (and visible) you are.

Attractors of People

Perhaps most important of all, people with the skill of visibility appear to have a certain magnetism that makes them the targets of

---

other people's friendly approaches. Psychologists call this a *'positive communication field'*.

What is a communication field? In physics, a field is 'an invisible set of forces which shapes the surrounding environment' - electromagnetic forces, for example. A communication field may be made up of hundreds of components: facial expressions, body positions, voice tone and choice of words, ways of using your eyes, ways of holding your head.

This cluster of mannerisms is difficult to analyze piece by piece, but the total effect is clearly visible to other people. We all know instinctively whether somebody likes us or doesn't like us. We know whether somebody is friendly or unfriendly, warm or cool. We can meet a total stranger and know in seconds whether the stranger does or does not want to spend more time with us. Organization contributors with visibility are those whose communication field is inviting and comfortable.

Paul Revere's Midnight Ride

Malcolm Gladwell,[60] in a recent book, gives us some fascinating information about Paul Revere's famous midnight ride that speaks directly to the concept of visibility:

> On the afternoon of April 18, 1776, a stable boy in Boston overheard one British officer say to another, something about "hell to pay tomorrow." The stable boy ran with the news to Boston's North End to the home of silversmith Paul Revere. Revere listened gravely. As the afternoon wore on Revere became convinced that the British were about to make the major move that had long been rumored - to march to Lexington, northwest of Boston to arrest the colonial leaders John Hancock and Samuel Adams, and then on to the town of Concord to seize the stores of guns and ammunition that some of the local colonial militia had stored there. What happened next has become part of historical legend. It was decided that the communities surrounding Boston had to be warned that the British were on their way so that the local militias could be roused to meet them. Revere was spirited

across Boston Harbor, jumped on a horse and began his 'midnight ride' to Lexington. In two hours he covered thirteen miles. In every town he passed through along the way he knocked on doors and spread the word, telling the local colonial leaders of the oncoming British and telling them to spread the word to others. Church bells started ringing, drums were beating, the news spread. Those informed sent out riders of their own, until alarms were going off all through the region. When the British finally started their march toward Lexington on the morning of the 19th, they were met, to their utter astonishment with organized and fierce resistance. In Concord that day, the British were confronted and soundly beaten by the colonial militia, and from that exchange came the American Revolution.

But here's the most interesting part of the story. Revere was not the only rider who set out from Boston that night. A fellow revolutionary - a tanner by the name of William Dawes - set out on the same urgent errand, working his way to Lexington via the towns west of Boston. He carried the identical message, through just as many towns and over just as many miles as Revere. But Dawes ride didn't set the countryside on fire. The local militia weren't alerted. In fact, so few men from one of the main towns he rode through - Waltham - fought the following day that some subsequent historians concluded that it must have been a strongly pro-British community. It wasn't. The people of Waltham just didn't find out the British were coming until it was too late.

Visibility Can Change History

What was the difference between the electrifying effect that Revere had as opposed to the inconsequentiality of Dawes? The difference was that Revere had a particular and rare set of social gifts that Dawes did not. He was gregarious and intensely social. It's not surprising that when Revere set out for Lexington that night, he would have known just how to spread the news as far and wide as possible. When he saw people on the road, he was so naturally social he would have stopped and told them. When he came upon a town, he would have known whose door to knock on, who the local militia leader was, and who the key players in town were. He had met most of them before. And they knew and respected him. Revere had *visibility*.

But William Dawes? He clearly had none of Revere's social gifts, because there is almost no record of anyone who remembers him that night. Dawes did not awaken the town fathers or militia commanders in the towns of Roxbury, Brookline, Watertown or Waltham. Why? Because Watertown, Roxbury, Brookline and Waltham were not Boston. And Dawes was likely a man with a normal social circle, which means that - like most of us - once he left his hometown, he probably wouldn't have known whose door to knock on.[55]

2. Being Known as Competent

"Power is not merely shouting aloud. Power is to act positively with all the components of power".

- Gamal Abdel Nasser

What Constitutes Useful Learning?

In 2004 an international network of researchers on learning [61] created an interdisciplinary group to study how individuals acquire the knowledge that makes them widely viewed as competent in their respective environments. A summary of ten years of research and development on learning at work was drawn up, and additional initiatives have been launched in the form of surveys designed to create an understanding of how competence develops.

Two areas of study quickly evolved:

- On one hand, there is a growing focus on *'situated learning'* - that is, learning under very distinct conditions and in clearly defined knowledge environments. This would include your technical knowledge of your specific job.
- A second discipline – *'informal learning'* - is the spontaneous and sometimes unforeseen learning that takes place during interaction with others, during change, or under other new conditions in everyday life and at work.

The interplay between formal technical education and the more spontaneous learning is thought to constitute *'useful learning'*: expertise associated with more than just an adaptation to prevailing structures, but rather with the ability to function effectively during changing conditions and in situations where broadly-based knowledge is required.

Beyond being 'known' by many, those with visibility are widely known as *competent*. They have shown that they can step in and deliver immediately. They have made the case that their experience is worth something. They are problem solvers - the 'rainmakers'.

They seem to enjoy being in the limelight and tend to make a good impression. They take the opportunity to tell others about their work and the work of their group, and they can effectively communicate what they know. They have gained the respect and confidence of individuals throughout the organization. They continue to develop those skills that will allow them to grow professionally. They radiate possibility, and their work seems to be guided by the question *"How can I contribute today"?* They enjoy competitive situations, difficult tasks, unique assignments, and high-visibility opportunities.

This is how our respondents described the individuals who displayed this skillset of visibility:

"He seeks out assignments that provide opportunities for his remarkable ability to be seen and to be recognized".

"If he lost his job today, he would have no problem quickly finding another. We would do whatever it took to keep from losing him".

"He has the ability to create a favorable impression and to gain the respect and confidence of all kinds of different people in this huge organization".

"When something needs to be done, we go to him".

"People have a very high opinion of her contribution".

"When he says something, people perk up and take notice".

"She knows everything there is to know about how this organization works. She pays attention and does her homework".

"Most people see her as the "go-to person" when critical information or action is needed".

3. *Being a Communicator of Ideas*

> *"There is nothing more difficult to take in hand, more perilous to conduct, or more uncertain in its success than to take the lead in the introduction of a new order of things".*
>
> — Jean-Jacques Rousseau

'*Practical Intelligence*': The Spotlight for Visibility

Personal visibility is a fertile mix of credibility plus a kind of 'street smarts' that allows clear and concise communication of ideas. Robert Sternberg,[62] a psychologist at *Yale University*, coined the term 'practical intelligence' to refer to the type of intelligence that enables one to function strategically in the real world: the ability to accurately read situations and to communicate effectively. Sternberg and his colleagues conducted a survey in which they asked people who were generally recognized as highly successful at their jobs to list behaviors they believed to be distinctly characteristic of particularly 'intelligent' people. The identified behaviors included: reasons logically and well, sees all aspects of a problem, gets to the heart of the problem, makes good decisions, and deals with problems resourcefully.

However, one grouping of skills stood out - one that seems to specifically describe *verbal ability*:
- is verbally fluent
- speaks clearly and articulately
- converses well
- is knowledgeable about a particular area or subject matter
- displays a good vocabulary
- interprets information accurately
- is a good source of ideas

Key organization contributors communicate what they know, and they inspire others. They are good at promoting ideas and creating enthusiasm. Clear communication = *credibility*. Whether you're an expert in information technology, cash accounting, or strategic planning, your task isn't merely to spout facts. It's to provide wisdom and insight. For a message to be understood and accepted, it has to be far enough out there to provide a jolt, but not so far out that it seems outlandish. It's important to be right, of course. But if you want to make an impact, you have to be provocative as well. You have to shake things up to be memorable. To some extent, you have to take the position, "Whether you agree with me or not, what I really want you to do is to rethink your position on this".

Often those with visibility are highly talented at both simplifying and exaggerating in ways that make ideas accessible. They have a remarkable ability to distill complex ideas into simple messages. What's their secret?   They communicate by using analogies, metaphors, and stories. If they're really talented, the guys on the factory floor, even the janitors, understand their pitch. Jack Welch went on the road, imploring managers to 'fix, close, or sell' businesses within *GE* that were not No. 1 or No. 2 in worldwide market share in their industry. Not a message that's easy to misunderstand.

The following quotes about significant contributors are typical and are drawn directly from our surveys:

> "He is quite verbally articulate and is expert at promoting ideas and creating enthusiasm for projects. He can talk easily and convincingly about what he does and what he and his group have accomplished".

> "She is great at communicating. She can talk easily and persuasively, and before you know it, you're on board with wherever she wants to go".

> "I'm continually amazed by the breadth of his knowledge - in every area".

> "In a group of people, she is not embarrassed to be called on to start a discussion or give an opinion about something she knows well".

"It seems easy for him to get favorable reactions from important people in the organization".

"He is obviously comfortable being in the limelight and has a great deal of charisma".

"Her ideas and opinions are always valued by others".

"He is successful at influencing the goals, activities, and processes at work".

4. Being the Center of a Knowledge Network

"Intelligence becomes an asset when some useful order is created out of free floating brainpower."
                                            - Thomas A. Stewart

---

Mavens Make a Difference

Let's listen to Malcolm Gladwell again. In *The Tipping Point*,[63] Gladwell identifies a type of organizational contributor he describes by use of the Yiddish word '*maven*', meaning 'one who accumulates knowledge'.

Not only does such a person accumulate knowledge, they do so obsessively. You may know someone like that. They pay attention. They remember. They tend to be curious about and interested in everything. And they're not just showing off. There is something reflexive and automatic about their acquisition of knowledge. They read more magazines, more newspapers, and what sets them apart is that they don't hoard this information for their own gain. They are motivated to pass it along because they want you to have it too. They are almost pathologically helpful - someone who wants to solve others' problems as well as their own.

A maven's motivation is to educate and to help. To be a maven is to be a teacher. But it is also to be a student. Mavens are really information brokers, sharing and trading what they know. They are data banks. They provide the information the organization needs to be most effective. Mavens are not necessarily distinguished by

---

status or even positions of power in the company (although those usually eventually come), but by the particular standing they have among their colleagues. They are widely recognized as indispensable.

Key contributors understand that information is power. They readily form alliances that put them in the know. They connect to others whose knowledge and expertise is valuable to the organization. Once they figure something out, they tell others about it. They see that knowledge is to be shared, not hoarded. Their helpfulness is quite obviously socially motivated and is connected to the prevailing orientation of *Collaboration* (see Chapter One). This desire to share knowledge differentiates them from 'brown-nosers' or 'braggarts'. They are driven by a desire to make the work of others easier, not by their own self-aggrandizing impulses. And this turns out to be an awfully effective way to get people's attention.

The following quotes about contributors are typical and are drawn directly from our surveys:

> "I'm continually amazed by the breadth of his knowledge - in every area".

> "He is an excellent mentor and has a wealth of wisdom and skills to impart to new people in the organization".

> "He is the technical expert in his area, but he also takes the time and effort to know something about everything that's important to our company".

> "She radiates possibility. Her watchwords seem to be: How am I going to contribute today"?

6. Continuous Résumé-ing

"Knowledge is the only meaningful resource".
- Peter Drucker

A Tip for Would-Be Organization Contributors from the Gospel of Matthew

In Biblical times, a 'talent' was a unit of money. These days, talent - accumulated knowledge and skill - and increasing your store of knowledge and updating your skills through continuous learning, is still the most relevant currency. Treat your wealth of knowledge as the wise servants did in the '*Parable of the Talents*' (*Matt.* 25:14–15). [64] Invest it and make it grow. If you bury it, as the fearful servant did, you'll lose your knowledge base and with it, your credibility.

Learn for a Lifetime

We used to think of school as grades K–12, with maybe a college degree or two stacked on top of that. Now we have to start thinking of school as K–80… in other words, as a lifelong process. The *National Research Council* [65] says that it used to take seven to 14 years for half of a worker's skills to become obsolete. Today it takes only three to five years for 50% of our knowledge to be outdated.

Playing the Contribution Game

Throughout American business history, the great majority of people never had to ask the question, "What should I contribute"? They were told what to contribute, and their tasks were dictated either by the work itself - as was the case for peasants or artisans - or by a master or mistress - as was the case for domestic servants. And until very recently it was taken for granted that most people were subordinates who did as they were told by those in power in the organization. No longer. Not in the knowledge economy. Now the question has become:

"What should my contribution be"?

The answer: What does the situation require? Given my strengths, my way of performing, and my values, how can I make the greatest contribution to what needs to be done? What results will have to be achieved to make a difference?

Key contributors embrace the mind-set of an independent contractor, even within their own organization. They know that to remain viable and indispensable in their companies, they must continually *'sharpen their saw'* - update their skills. They have made the choice to grow, both personally and professionally. The most effective of the contributors identified in our surveys continually asked themselves the following kinds of questions:

- "Which of my skills are most valuable to the organization"?
- "Where can I add value to the organization even though this may not be in the job I currently hold"?
- "How have I demonstrated my value lately"?
- "Who among my customers will testify to it"?
- "What evidence is there that my skills are state-of-the-art"?
- "What do I need to learn to be more effective"?
- "Will my year-end resume look different than last year's"?
- "How can I contribute today"?

Contributors seek opportunities for their competence to be seen and recognized. They radiate possibility and create a sense of *'It can be done'* in the organization.

The following quotes about organization contributors are typical and are drawn directly from our surveys:

"If there's a new technology on the horizon or a new wrinkle in our business, he knows something about it".

"It sounds like a cliché, but her focus truly seems to be on adding value".

"People have a very high opinion of her contribution".

"He carefully monitors and seeks to improve his own performance, even beyond the requirements of particular assignments".

Action Stance

Initiative

Mental Agility

Action Learning

Receptive Nature

Collaboration

Visibility

Do You Have What It Takes to Make Your Competence Visible?

It's time to test your *'Visibility'*. Do you possess this important capability? Take this short quiz and find out. For each set of descriptors, those on the right of the page and those on the left, check the ones that apply to you. Check as many items as are descriptive of your work style. Your task here is to make as honest an assessment of your skills as possible. The results will help you to understand how natural this ability is for you and, if you choose, guide you to activities and exercises designed to develop the skill of visibility.

☐	I tend to associate with a few close friends at work.	☐	I am generally well-liked and have developed a wide network of friends and acquaintances.
☐	I prefer to let others mention my accomplishments and comment on my contribution.	☐	I am able to talk easily about what I do and what I have accomplished.
☐	I often feel intimidated around people with greater experience or seniority than I.	☐	I usually feel comfortable with senior people (those with greater experience, age, or authority than I), and I can express my views in a straightforward manner.
☐	I tend to be somewhat reserved, and it takes me a while to get to know people at work.	☐	I have the ability to make a strong and positive impact on the majority of people I meet.
☐	I am a diligent worker, but I am still seeking to master all the aspects of my job.	☐	I am viewed by people at work as "the expert" in my area.
☐	I find that others in the work setting often don't know where I work or what exactly it is I do for the organization.	☐	Most people at work have a high opinion of my contribution and often comment on it.
☐	I have a hard time getting heard or getting my ideas across in meetings.	☐	My ideas and opinions are usually highly valued by others.
☐	I worry about being laid-off and being able to find another job that is as good as the one I have now.	☐	If I lost my job today, I could easily find another.
☐	I usually don't feel comfortable talking in front of a group of people.	☐	In a group of people, I would not be embarrassed to be called upon to start a discussion or give an opinion about something I know well.

☐ I understand the issues and projects very well, but I tend not to try and force my opinions on others.	☐ I am able to easily persuade others and influence others.
☐ I communicate best with other technical experts in my area of work.	☐ I can make my positions understood even to people who haven't shared my work experience.
☐ I am considered a hard worker, and I don't spend much time talking about the issues at work.	☐ I am known for my critical thinking skills and my precise thought.
☐ I know quite a bit about my own work group, but I don't usually inquire about how other areas and individuals work.	☐ When people need information about the organization and its workings, they often come to me.
☐ My work contacts are generally confined to my specific technical area.	☐ I have networked extensively both inside and outside the organization, and I know the people who possess key information.
☐ My primary work relationships are with those at my level and below in the organization.	☐ I have been able to keep up good relationships with people at all levels in the organization.
☐ I am known as the "expert" in my specific work area.	☐ I am highly skilled in my area, but I also take the time and effort to know something about everything that is important to my company.
☐ I prefer to work in areas and on tasks that I know well.	☐ I most enjoy jobs that challenge my abilities, even including tasks that I have never done before.

☐ I am most concerned about making sure that my stated goals and objectives are met.	☐ I appropriately pursue goals even beyond what is required or expected in my current job.
☐ I concentrate on demonstrating excellence in my technical area.	☐ I am concerned with developing skills in new areas that may eventually relate to my industry.
☐ I am focused on doing my present job to the best of my ability.	☐ I seek out opportunities for accomplishment and advancement.
− _____ **Total Boxes Checked**	+ _____ **Total Boxes Checked**

Our survey results indicate that over 68% of respondents mentioned some aspect of what we have come to call *'Visibility'*. Recall that our respondents were either key organization contributors themselves or managers who had the task of selecting employees to play a prominent role in their organizations in times of difficulty or crisis, or anticipated growth. They occupied all levels of the organization, from executives to individual contributors. In every case, the respondents were asked to comment on those skills that they believed made employees indispensable to their companies.

Add the numbers in the Totals boxes together, retaining their arithmetic sign. If your score is between -20 and -10, your visibility is underdeveloped. You may be hampered by an assumption that 'good work speaks for itself '- a significant handicap in an organizational environment where those who are considered indispensable must be widely recognized as competent. Your visibility would be increased by attending to and practicing the exercises and activities in the next section of this chapter.

If your total score is between +10 and +20, it is likely that your competence is highly visible in your organization. Nevertheless, you may wish to review the exercises and activities in the next section of this chapter to assist you in further developing your visibility.

Make Your Competence Known to Those Who Count

Lean organizations dictate a new reality: that leaders are needed at every level of the company. Looking up the organization for leadership just doesn't work anymore. Business is changing too rapidly. Top executives must be able to clearly identify and make use of *all* the talent that exists in the organization - or face the consequences in the worldwide marketplace. The era of doing good work but toiling in obscurity is gone. In today's organization, global competition, job instability, and economic uncertainty require something more. Build a name for yourself as a problem-solver and a contributor, and you'll be a valuable person to have around.

If you want to add to your capability in the area of visibility, here are some how-to's to help you sharpen this skillset.

As you read through the Skill Builders associated with each aspect of visibility, circle the symbol beside those you would like to implement as part of your *Key Contributor Ready Kit*. Then use Table 6 in the Appendix to fill out aspects of your '*Visibility Kit*'.

1. *Being Widely Known in the Organization*

At the most basic level, one becomes visible in an organization because he or she is social. Remember, being widely known in your organization is the first step to being indispensable. It's not the *only* step, but it's the *first* step. It's all about developing a winning style and cultivating relationships that can be instrumental in opening doors you never dreamed could open for you.

Start by Being Approachable

Sometimes people look around and believe that in order to increase their social support, they will have to entirely change their life patterns. Usually drastic changes are not needed. For example, watch those who have difficulty connecting with others. You see them hurrying to meetings, on the elevator, off the elevator, eyes front, every inch of their bodies clearly communicating that they are in a hurry and that you delay them at your peril. These habits can become pervasive, carrying over into your behavior even in situations where there are people who you would like to get to know better.

Skill Builders:

☼ Slow down. Facially and physically focus on the folks who are also going into or out of that meeting. Try gathering your papers together less swiftly, looking around, making eye contact, following up on a remark that someone makes about their vacation or other personal information. This will not produce instantaneous social success, but it will communicate that you are interested in the individuals as people, and over time personal contact may well grow from there.

☼ To be approachable, you often have to initiate the transaction. Put out your hand first, make the first eye contact, share the first piece of information.

☼ When you're at an event, act like the host. Be gracious and interested. Smile and look people in the eye. Be sensitive to body language. If you notice a person at a gathering who seems to be alone, bring them into the center of things. If you are the leader of an organization, you'll have an eager and committed worker for life. People remember special treatment.

☼ Have a planned and prepared self-introduction that makes you a person of interest.

☼ Read the newspaper and industry periodicals or watch news reports and have at least three things you can talk about. Create a 'small-talk notebook' containing anecdotes and questions you jot down about life or current events that are guaranteed to stimulate conversation. Be creative - or even outrageous - but always professional with your ideas.

Δ Listen. Approachable people are good at listening. They listen without interrupting. They ask clarifying questions, they don't instantly judge, they listen to understand.

☼ Disclose some personal information about yourself. It's hard for people to relate to an enigma.

☼ Personalize others. Approachable people work to know and remember important things about the people they work with. Know three things about everybody - their interests or their children - something you can chat about other than the business agenda.

Δ Appreciate the magic of questions. Many people don't ask enough curiosity questions when in their work mode.

Questions show you are interested in others or their viewpoints and make you approachable. "What if ..."; "What are you thinking ..."; "How do you see that"? Ask more questions than others and keep probing until you understand.

☼   Initiate personal follow-ups. Congratulate someone on a presentation well made. Make a request for additional information that includes mention that you were pleased to see the person at the last meeting. You'll show that you are someone who really cares about the work of the others in your company.

☼   Always be 'present'. Make yourself known one way or another through articles, books, e-zines, workshops, classes, speeches, e-mail, printed newsletters, public appearances, networking events, or even via personal note.

These are simple steps that are made almost automatically by those who are 'people focused'.

They are skills that need to be learned by the more 'task focused' among us who yearn for more social contact. They may appear to be normal networking skills, but in fact they are more person-focused than much of the networking that is done in business situations.

Put Yourself Out There

A great many people identify themselves as 'shy'. So how do you push through that? You do it by being fully prepared and networking strategically.

Skill Builders:

♘   Find the *'fast flow'* [66.] Go where events are flowing the fastest. Surround yourself with a churning mass of people and things happening. Those who are lucky get acquainted with everyone in sight. Don't let yourself become isolated.

179

☼   Network internally so others get to know you and your accomplishments. Never underestimate the power of 'doing lunch'. Make the rounds in your office building and connect with the movers and shakers.

☼   Keep plenty of business cards to hand out to that person you just met for a minute in the elevator that might collaborate with you on something important down the line.

☼   Volunteer for high-profile assignments. Join a company committee or volunteer to take on extra projects. Being proactive will ensure that your positive reputation spreads beyond your department. Let your management know of your commitment and desire to contribute.

☼   Speak up in meetings. Request clarification of someone else's idea or, better yet, offer up one of your own. It's the only way your superiors will ever remember you attended. And while you're at it, come down on the side of *how* it can be done - not why it can't.

☼   Make presentations - the absolute best way to get the eyes and ears of the power brokers.

☼   Join the club. There's a professional organization for virtually every field. Mere membership doesn't give you wheeler-dealer status. But check out this story:

> Bob Wooten, cofounder of *Wooten-Jackson*, a Boston management consulting firm, is a member of the *Massachusetts Organization Development Network*. He recently joined the group's program committee. His first task: call CEOs to invite them to speaking engagements - not a bad way to meet wheeler-dealers.

△   Pass articles along with a note if you come across one that may be of interest to a coworker or colleague. Have a small card printed up with the message: "I thought you might find the enclosed of interest," with your name, company name, and contact information. Be the eyes of your colleagues who may not have the time to read all the professional literature you do. You'll provide a valuable and unforgettable service that they will undoubtedly appreciate.

☼ Pay attention to special occasions (honors, appointments, promotions) and stay in touch. Write e-mails and make quick check-in phone calls to people you want to do business with. Go through your network list periodically and contact those people you want to remember you. Keep your name and your company's name in front of them.

☼ Get to know the support staff (secretaries, admins, assistants) of the person or company you may want to do business with. It costs you nothing to develop these relationships and, when you call, there will be a better chance of your being put right through.

☼ Selectively donate your services to nonprofit organizations that may be in need of your expertise. Set the stage for people to get to know who you are and what you do.

☼ Jobs on the boundaries between organizational units or between the company and the outside world have great visibility. They often become 'power positions'.

☼ Another good way to gain visibility is by working on task forces and powerful committees. However, the most impactful activities have to be relevant and solve pressing organizational problems.

One Good Turn Deserves Another

Social scientists who have spent a good part of their careers studying its effects point out that one of the most potent weapons of influence at our disposal is the *'rule of reciprocity'*. [67] The rule says, in effect, that an almost automatic human response is that we try to repay, in kind, whatever another person has provided us. If someone does us a favor, we try to do one for them in return. If someone sends us a birthday present, we try to remember them on their birthday as well.

If a couple invites us to a party, we invite them, in turn, to one of ours. By virtue of the reciprocity rule, we feel almost obligated to the future repayments of such kindnesses. So typical is it for indebtedness to accompany the receipt of such favors, 'much obliged' has become a synonym for thank-you, not only in the English language but in other languages as well. Noted paleontologist Richard Leakey suggests that the essence of what makes us human is the reciprocity system. He claims that we are human because our ancestors learned to share food and skills 'in an honored network of obligation'. Cultural anthropologists view this 'web of indebtedness' as a unique adaptive mechanism of human beings, allowing for the division of labor, the exchange of diverse forms of goods and services, and the creation of interdependencies that bind individuals together in highly efficient units.[68]

How can you use the reciprocity rule to your advantage without being conniving? For the people you care about and those who are important to you (and this includes your boss), consider creating a series of 'interest-bearing accounts'. In a nutshell, this means that any relationship can be looked at like an account in which there are deposits and withdrawals. If you are a 'taker', always asking for something from others, your 'account' will be 'overdrawn' when it comes time for you to make a 'withdrawal' - to ask for something you really need. But if you have made adequate deposits into these accounts from time to time, there will be ample resources available from others when you really need them: in times of crisis or for an important project.

Δ What kinds of deposits can you make into the accounts of people who are important to you? How can you make sure you have ample 'reserves' when you need to make a withdrawal?

- Find out your boss's priorities and commit to doing things that make his or her life easier. For example, take his place on a committee or gather up the numbers she needs for the next budget round.
- Cultivate a reputation as someone who rallies around your colleagues' objectives and as someone who makes results happen. This will gain you a reputation as a person of action, so that when you do have a need

or a request, it will be taken a bit more seriously by colleagues, and your manager may well pay-it-forward by granting you greater authority to act, increased responsibilities, or plum assignments.

2. Being Known as Competent

Being widely known in your organization is the first step to being indispensable. More important still is being considered 'competent'. And not just competent in your technical area… competent generally, across-the-board - someone to go to when a coworker needs answers, advice, or just a good sounding board.

If your goal is to be seen as competent and indispensable in your organization, it makes sense to develop a stockpile of skills, knowledge, and accomplishments that add value. But for activities to 'enhance value', they must attract the notice of other people. Few people excel by quietly going about doing their job. Twenty years ago, a company worker could be obscure yet secure. Not anymore. Today your competence must be visible to those who are in power positions. What this means at the bottom line is simply becoming 'an established expert with good PR', according to Tom Peters. Peters, speaker, consultant, and author of *In Search of Excellence* and *The Pursuit of WOW,*[69] advises positioning yourself as an *'organizational guru'*.

Skill Builders:

☼ Specialize. An organizational guru is the one who knows all about a particular expertise - whether it's how to deal with export/import issues in Brazil, team building with accountants, or the idiosyncrasies of a particular supplier or major customer. A guru is someone who, anytime there is a question about licenses, people say, *'See Bob on the fifteenth floor'*. To be a guru, it helps not to dig wide, but deep. Although organizations appreciate a wide-ranging knowledge base, 'guru' status can be achieved as well through a deep technical groove. Know what you're good at, what you're passionate about, and stick to it. Carve out your niche that separates your business or enterprise from the competition. Gurus are only as good as their credibility.

Δ   Become an expert. Individuals who become indispensable in carrying out a certain aspect of the company's function will usually be promoted, even if a new title has to be created for the position. If you are developing expertise on a particular project, make your superiors aware of your special knowledge and the extent to which people depend on you to provide that knowledge. Or, if there is an area in which you feel that your department is sorely lacking, why don't you be the one to fill this knowledge gap? When you do, you'll reap the rewards of indispensability.

☼   Develop a 'credibility anchor'. It may be a research report, a book, a series of articles, a signature speech, or a defined area of influence. Whatever it is, it 'anchors' your credibility in your subject matter.

☼   Create a 'niche'. You can develop your own niche by picking up a skill or technical knowledge that is vital to your company, yet relatively hard to learn. Be the best at something that no one else wants to do, and you will dramatically raise your level of importance to your organization.

☼   Walk the talk. Trade shows, conferences, networking events, all offer opportunities to test-market your brand. Dress the part and tell others who you are. If you act the part long enough, you will become your desired brand. The sacred trinity to achieving brand-dominance is: *consistency, authenticity, clarity.* Make sure you have customers who can attest to your skills.

☼   Score the points. Gurus need sizable resumes and litanies of achievement. They need, in other words, to be *known for something*, whether it's saving $100,000 in production costs or creating the company's tightest product-development schedule. There have to be stories associated with your name. You might have the world's most scintillating personality, but at the end of the day, people will judge you by looking at your stuff. P.S: Timing helps. Often the 'guru' is simply the one who had the good idea first.

☼   Write articles about your work for trade journals, industry publications, or newsletters. If important people in your field notice your work, so will your boss.

☼   Volunteer to speak at industry or association meetings. Then let your boss know you will be speaking and ask if there is specific information he would like covered.

☼   Get mentors. Mentors may not sell you to others, but they can give you the confidence to sell yourself. You need honest feedback. With it you can more ably steer down the path of your real expertise. According to one study, people with mentors become better and faster decision makers, given that they can always call on another's expertise. Associate with people who will motivate you to improve and excel. Create a personal board of advisors who can counsel, guide, and inspire you. Select organizationally powerful people if you can. With a wide range of contacts, you will have access to people who have the capacity to help when needed. Don't waste time on the wrong people - the 'energy vampires' who drain you of energy, enthusiasm, and ideas.

Δ   Work on your own mentoring skills, so that it is clear to top management that you have wisdom/skills to impart to fledglings. People who develop those under them are always seen as valuable. They are not only sending dozens of effective people into the organization, they are also creating allies everywhere.

Δ   Communicate what you know. Every corporate office has its political hack. He's the one who hoards information, looks for credit, self-promotes, and hogs the spotlight. But the real guru gets ahead by giving it away. The real gurus and leaders understand that the essence of management is getting things done through other people. If someone asks you for information, provide it yourself... or track it down. Pass on

185

tidbits of information you think will help people do their jobs better or broaden their perspective and understanding. You will become known as the *'go-to person'*.

☼ Take a minute to be remarkable. After you've done what you were called upon to do, take the last few seconds that you touch the project to distinguish yourself. Go one better than anyone else does. Do even one thing more than is the standard operating procedure in your position. If you've prepared a report to send off to someone else, give 'em a call to make sure they received it and to 'answer any quick questions' they might have about it. When you leave your biggest customer's office, make it a point to stop by the secretary's or receptionist's desk to say good-bye. When you're leaving a meeting, if you're walking away with something of value, tell the person who provided the tidbit that you appreciate their contribution and why it meant something to you. It won't take you long to be the one people remember (in a good way).

Want to be Seen as Competent? Understand That You Already Are... and Believe It

There is some discomfort in most of us that makes us reluctant to take credit for our accomplishments or to even accept a well-deserved compliment. Try an experiment. Give someone you know a genuine compliment about a quality they have or about something they have done that you truly appreciate. Often their first response is to downplay their contribution or their effort: "Oh, I was just doing my job." "Anyone would have done the same thing." "It was nothing." What is it that makes us uneasy about accepting credit for something wonderful we have done? We feel proud of our accomplishments and our skills, but we don't know how to take credit for them gracefully, without seeming like a braggart or a know-it-all.

Author and consultant Peggy Klaus has written a charming how-to book on this very topic: *Brag: The Art of Tooting Your Own Horn Without Blowing It* [70] In it she advises creating a *'bragologue'* - a

---

list of your abilities and accomplishments designed to clarify in your own mind exactly what you do have to offer.

☼   Make a list of your abilities and accomplishments.
- What would you and others say are your five personality pluses?
- What are the ten most interesting things you have done or have happened to you?
- What do you like/love about your current job/career?
- How does your job/career use your skills and talents, and what projects are you working on right now that best showcases them?
- What career successes are you most proud of having accomplished?
- What new skills have you learned in the last year?
- What obstacles have you overcome to get where you are today, both professionally and personally, and what essential lessons have you learned from some of your mistakes?
- What training and education have you completed, and what did you gain from those experiences?
- In what ways are you making a difference in people's lives?

You don't have to start right off by broadcasting these to others. But just the act of clarifying them for yourself will make it easier for you to be in touch with what skills you bring to the party.

The One-Minute Definition

Your accomplishments and your abilities, communicated in a concise, vivid fashion, can do more to focus your credibility than any long-winded speech or explanation.

☼   Develop a one-sentence, one-minute definition of what you have to offer (or want to offer) the world: a one-sentence marketing plan. That one sentence carefully thought out will point you in the right direction and help focus all your efforts.

☼   Make it realistic. Acknowledge your current position and focus on the future.

☼   Make a list of what you have already done. Keep the list in chronological order, divided by month, over the span of a year. At the end of the year, you can see what you have and have not achieved.

☼   An 'accomplishments' list also helps you determine whether you are making the kind of professional and personal progress you have in mind for yourself. If you have a clear picture of your accomplishments, you are way ahead in terms of letting your boss know why you should have that raise or promotion.

☼   Write ten different statements of competence that you would not consider arrogant if spoken by someone else, but that apply to you. Practice saying them proudly. After all, if it would be acceptable for someone else to say, then it is acceptable for you!

Trust and Perceived Competence Go Hand in Hand

People rated as highly trustworthy are also generally rated as highly competent. How can you behave in ways that will facilitate trust? Certain key behaviors seem to contribute to whether or not others see you as trustworthy.

Δ   Examining your daily actions with the following questions in mind will enhance your reputation as someone trustworthy:

- Is my behavior predictable or erratic? If your behavior is confusing, indecisive, or inconsistent, others cannot depend on you to behave in certain ways in similar situations. They cannot make reasonable hypotheses about how you might react under new or different circumstances. Some degree of predictability or consistency is required in order for people to believe in you. Consistency means that the same personal values and organizational aims will influence what you say and do, that your preoccupation with quality or customer service, for example, will not give way to shifting tides of fashion or politics.

- Do I communicate clearly and ceaselessly? Sometimes we make statements about our intentions, even if tentative in our own minds, without realizing that to others these are viewed as promises. If you frequently make statements that you don't intend as commitments but that others might reasonably interpret as such, they may well believe that you're unreliable. If you are clear about what you mean, there's less chance that others will find your statements misleading.

- Do I treat promises seriously or lightly? If we treat our own commitment seriously, others will too. If we take our promises lightly, others will also. Problems arise when people have different perceptions of the importance of both your word and the circumstances required to justify not keeping your promise. Further complications arise when people can't distinguish between wishes or vague promises on your part and those ideas to which you are seriously committed.

189

- Am I forthright or dishonest? If you knowingly mislead or lie, for example, making a promise you never intended to keep, then other people have good reason not to trust you. There is no such thing as a little bit of dishonesty. Discovering that someone has been deceitful casts doubt over everything he or she says or does. Honesty doesn't require full disclosure. It does, however, require a clear indication of areas about which complete candor should not be expected and an explanation of why it is not appropriate. Still, greater disclosure between people generally makes for better working relationships and easier resolution of problems should they arise.

Being Trustworthy Means Taking Responsibility

Being willing to take responsibility when appropriate goes farther than perhaps any other quality in building trust with others.

Δ   Be honest and open with colleagues and your manager. If problems emerge with work for which you are responsible, tell your peers and your manager immediately. It also pays to suggest a solution.

Δ   Admit any mistake early and inform everyone affected what could occur because of it.

Δ   Publicly acknowledge the mistake, if necessary, and take personal responsibility.

Δ   Demonstrate what you have learned so the mistake does not happen again.

Δ   Move on. Don't dwell on it.

Connect Upwards in Your Organization to Leverage Your Visibility and Impact

☼ Connect upwards in the organization to leverage your visibility and impact. Make it a point to have a conversation with your boss (or someone higher-up) whenever the opportunity presents itself.

☼ Practice relating comfortably with the 'power brokers'. Associate yourself with the stars, not the whiners. Invite them to lunch. Walk by their office a lot. Ask for advice. Get to know and connect with those in the organization who hold the reins.

☼ Schedule regular meetings with your manager to assess your achievements and progress, and be sure you are prepared to show off a little.

☼ Let your management know of your commitment and desire to contribute. Make yourself known through the established procedures. Send an e-mail that softly touts your accomplishments through 'status reports'. Communicate positive progress by using such language as: "Let me update you on what we have accomplished ..."

☼ If possible, find ways to work on projects with your boss. Volunteer for high-profile tasks, special projects, or committees, even if they are risky. When you show how your daily tasks affect the company, you show an awareness of your company's goals and vision, and that you are on top of your daily activities.

☼ Become indispensable - perform critical functions and develop critical relationships. As a result, you will be well taken care of by your manager.

Δ Help your manager. Give him or her what they need to perform most effectively. Identify what's important. Get to know your manager's work style so you can communicate more effectively. Verbally communicate potential risks management should be aware of. Surface and address the issues, and you will get credit for thinking "big picture".

☼   Send your CEO informal notes or articles of interest. This lets him know you are always thinking of new ideas and that you have a genuine enthusiasm and concern for the company.

☼   Your performance review is one time you can count on to have uninterrupted face time with your boss. Make the most of it. Use your performance review to establish your value to the company.

- Take control of your review. Keep track of the necessary data and it as a springboard for discussion. Keep detailed records of your accomplishments. List everything that benefited the company. Include the kinds of things that would go on a resume. Where possible, translate each accomplishment into a dollar value to the company. Your boss may know about your accomplishments, but may have never seen them tied together, listed in one place at one particular time. Your boss has never devoted as much time thinking about you as you have. The company is making a profit off you, and you want this to be noticed in order to realize that you are providing a tremendous return on the company's investment in you. Your boss needs to know that you appreciate constructive critiques because you care about your job and want to do it better.

- You can schedule short, regular meetings between you and your manager so that you both know what needs to be done. Ask your boss what you should be doing more of and what skills you should acquire. Use this opportunity to tell your boss about your goals for the coming months and how you will track your progress. Ask what you can do to make yourself more valuable to the company. You accomplish two things with this straightforward approach. You let the boss know you are moving ahead, and you will discover what specific actions you need to take to move ahead - taking a course, getting a degree, or handling extra projects. Give specific recommendations to increase the company's productivity. Provide facts and figures about staffing requirements, budgets, and whatever else is required to put your ideas into action. Put your recommendations in writing, preferably to more than one person. Send them to your boss first. Send a copy to the personnel department. Even if your suggestions are not adopted, your effort will look good on your record when review time rolls around. Sell your accomplishments to the person who can make a difference in your career.

Play the "Contribution Game" Rather than the "Success Game"

When we play the 'success game', life looks like an obstacle course in which our task is to overcome hurdle after hurdle. Another performance mode is that of *'radiating possibility'*: "How can I contribute today"? That way we see ourselves as part of a team of human beings - which gives our life relevance *and* visibility! You want to be a person 'on a mission' who has the company's (and your colleagues') best interests at heart.

Δ   Can you look for new business? Develop new ideas and projects.

Δ   Can you learn a new skill that will help you in the future?

Δ   If you have a better idea about how to do something, implement it! Don't just talk about it.

Δ   Commit yourself to providing better service to your internal customers than your 'competition'.

Δ   Anticipate problems and solve them before they arise. Take the initiative and learn much more than your job requires.

Δ   Become an expert in a critical area. Become someone to whom your colleagues turn regularly. Become a resource and an inspiration.

Δ   People who are savvy work from the outside in. Determine the demand characteristics or requirements of each situation and each person you face and select from among your various skills to find the best approach to make things work in that circumstance.

Δ   Be accessible. Make yourself available. Check in frequently with colleagues, help others at staff meetings, join committees, contribute ideas, and give people the opportunity to know and respect you.

Δ   When the boss is away, add to your indispensability dramatically by completing jobs she assigned before she departed. There is nothing a manager appreciates more after a trip than "Here's that job you wanted. It's done".

See yourself as a 'service center' within your organization. Sharpen your insights into your personal 'marketplace'. And you'll see exactly what you have to do to make yourself indispensable. There are both internal and external customers. Other departments, several people in your own functional area, your direct supervisor - these are your clients and customers. Unless you take pains to provide the best possible service and do so at a competitive price, they'll replace you with a better service provider. In essence, somebody else will steal your business. Seek regular and direct contact with your 'customers', build strong relationships with them, deliver the highest quality service possible, anticipate their needs, and develop a reputation for responsiveness. Your customers are your only source of job security.

2. *Being a Clear Communicator of Ideas*

The best idea in the world is useless if it can't be communicated in a way that others can understand it. "I'm sure he's brilliant, but I don't understand a thing he says", won't get you too far when it comes to others seeking you out for your wisdom and your insight. "Brilliant but useless" is the phrase that comes to mind. You have to be able to make yourself understood to people who haven't shared your life experiences or your technical training. Organizations are moving away from homogeneity toward diversity. You have to be able to speak from more than just your own worldview. You have to be able to create bridges of thought.

Skill Builders:

☼   Master the art of conveying yourself in a winning way. Know how to convey your strengths, expertise, success, reputation, and influence, even when your target audience reaches beyond your local community (where you can be seen and experienced in person) and extends nationally or internationally via telephone, conference call, tele-classes, or e-mail.

☼   Join a *Toastmasters*-type group. This is not just a way to sharpen your speaking and communication skills, but a way to master the art of thinking on your feet, feeling comfortable with your own ideas and your ability to communicate them effectively -essential for the contributor who seeks visibility.

☼   Create and rehearse a compelling 30-second message for any project on which you are working. Develop a pitch that captures the highlights of who you are, what you do, and what value you add to the enterprise. Focus on the most interesting aspect of what you do. Be prepared to deliver your promo any time you meet someone you don't know who seems interested. Be especially ready should you encounter your boss's boss or some other bigwig in the elevator, hallway, or parking lot. If they don't know who you are and what you do, how will they remember you when you want them to?

☼   Make your points clear and concise enough that they can be delivered effectively to others while walking down the hall to the conference room, eating lunch, or riding up in the elevator.

☼   'Walk your talk'. And just as important... 'Believe your walk'. Be passionate, and it shows. This skyrockets credibility.

☼   Have a consistent message that you send and be confident in what you are doing.

Effective communication underlies all forms of 'leadership'. In organizations, this doesn't have to be job-title-dictated leadership. More importantly, it's *influence-based* leadership. Organizations require more leadership at every level as the organization is involved in higher degrees of innovation. As organizations embrace change, there have to be people who can explain the changes and persuade others to go along with them. Expert communication skills are important because you have to make yourself understood to people who haven't shared your life experiences. As organizations move away from homogeneity toward diversity, there is a need for people who are more cosmopolitan, who don't speak simply from within a single worldview, but who can understand and create bridges of thought.

Key Contributors Are Verbally Agile when Presenting a Case for Change

Buying into the new way of doing things also involves buying into letting go of the old way. These are two different actions, both necessary but not sufficient by themselves. Both require an educational component. Contributors are experts at educating others about how the new approach solves the problem.

Δ   Make your communications stand out. Corporate America sends out seven billion e-mails a day. Give your messages must-read subject lines (but only if they *are* must-read). Consider the employee who was requesting a meeting with her boss to discuss a cost-saving plan and sent an e-mail entitled: "You bring the coffee, I'll bring the $2 million".

☼   Change the language you use. For example, the word 'experiment' is much safer than 'business plan'. Properly set up, experiments should never fail. Rather, they should prove or disapprove the hypothesis and provide useful information. The learning from an experiment can be adjusted and cycled back into the thinking so that, over time, assumptions are changed. Business plans, on the other hand, are much riskier, because they are either met or not met. Business plans that do not meet their objectives are usually killed.

Δ   Help your organization gain as much learning as possible before formal go-no go decisions are made. When trying to sell your breakthrough idea to your management team, using the right language can help you increase the likelihood that your idea will be accepted, and mitigate the risks if, for some reason, your experiment doesn't succeed. Skillful use of language gets you noticed.

Charismatic Contributors Have an Innate Ability to Size Up Their Audience Quickly and Pick the Right Strategy to Captivate, Persuade, and Inspire

If asked how they do it, they probably couldn't tell you. They just know the right things to say. Fortunately for the rest of us, there has been some focused research on the best ways to structure a message to move any audience in the direction of not only agreeing with what we have to say, but trusting us in the bargain.[71]

Imagine categorizing all the stakeholders in your enterprise along two independent dimensions:

- *Agreement* - whether they agree or disagree with your point of view or the direction in which you are headed.
- *Trust* - whether or not they believe you tell the truth and are honest about what is happening, including your own actions. And whether you trust them.

Once you have diagnosed where each of your stakeholders stands in this model, you can create an influence strategy to manage your coalition and support-building efforts. The goal is obviously to move everyone in the direction of increasing agreement and trust - in essence, making them all '*Allies*'. Charismatic individuals understand that a well-articulated vision and authentic behavior in support of that vision is the best way to gain the support of others. However, the specific influence strategy you choose depends on where your audience falls in the initial diagnostic framework.

Allies - those high on agreement with you and whom you trust. These individuals share your vision, goals, and approach. These are people to whom you feel you can tell the whole truth without any concern that the knowledge will somehow come back to haunt you. The basic strategy with Allies is to maintain the relationship at the same level of support or greater.

☼ Skill Builders for Use with Allies:

- Reaffirm and reinforce their commitment with vivid testimonials and impressive results. Use dramatic examples to intensify their commitment.
- Reaffirm the quality of the relationship. They need to hear what it is they are doing that is making a positive difference. If they are already 'actively' supportive, you will want to keep them active by finding additional ways they can contribute. If they are Allies - that is, in general agreement - but not doing anything active to support the cause, give them some direction and clear action they can take. Stress the 'unfinished business' yet to be done. Let them know what you need from them.
- Ask for advice and support. Because they are your Allies, they can give you good advice and feedback. They can see the field clearly, evaluate your perceptions, and provide information on where the other players in the game stand.

Opponents - those with whom you share an honest relationship (trust is high), but who disagree with you or have conflicting purposes, direction, goals, or methods.

☼ Skill Builders for Use with Opponents:

- Reaffirm the quality of the relationship and the fact that it is based on trust. Tell them the reason you value their friendship is because you know they will be honest and tell you the truth every step of the way.
- Acknowledge your purpose, your vision, and your goals, and be direct about what you are trying to do.
- State in a neutral way what you believe their position is (so as to make sure you understand it correctly).
- Encourage them to learn more about your position by inviting questions and requests for clarification. Stress areas of agreement and common ground.

- Engage in some form of mutual problem solving. Examine the alternatives and their consequences. Avoid making any important statements without clear evidence to back them up. Show them where your information comes from. Use only information from experts and authorities they will recognize and respect. Negotiate knowing that because the quality of the relationship is strong, you will find a way to reach an agreement. Ask for a little and get it, rather than asking for a lot and being turned down. Try to achieve some partial commitment to get them used to agreeing on smaller issues. Then they will be more inclined to help you later with something more important. The value of these interactions with Opponents is that they can challenge what you are doing to make you personally stronger and your plan more effective.

Backslappers - those who appear in agreement with you on how to proceed, but with whom you have a low degree of trust. These are people who seem aligned with your vision, goals, and objectives, but who usually don't give you the whole story when you have contact with them. The issue with them is one of trust, not one of agreement.

☼   Skill Builders for Use with Backslappers:

- Reaffirm the agreement. State your purpose, goals, and objectives, and affirm the fact that they have gone on record as supporting those things. Acknowledge and value the support you have received from them with regard to the substance of your activities.
- Acknowledge that caution exists. You need to put into words that there is some reservation on your part as to how honest and direct the dialogue has been in the past. The key is to talk about the difficulty in the relationship, rather than suggesting that the difficulty is the other person. Acknowledge your own contribution to the difficulty and your wish to find a way of moving ahead in spite of the caution that exists.

- Be clear about what you want in working together. You want them to give you more than just lip service. The key is to be clear about what you want, not in terms of projects or goals, but in terms of how you work together. Use dramatic examples. You want the other person to *feel* as well as think.
- Ask the other person what they want or need from you. The more they can express any reservation or disappointment they have had in dealing with you, the better the hope for the future. Trust is extremely fragile. It can take years to develop and moments to destroy.
- Try to build some agreement about how to work together. Even if they take a small step in your direction, it's easier to move them to bigger agreements later.

Fence-Sitters - those individuals who will not take a stand either for you or against you. At the end of a meeting with them, you are never quite sure what has been decided. The Fence-Sitter is a bureaucratic prototype. You experience a huge drain of energy in dealing with their being so resigned to caution. It's hard to trust a Fence-Sitter, and agreement with them evaporates with the slightest breeze.

☼ Skill Builders for Use with Fence-Sitters:

- Try to smoke them out and find out where they stand. Encourage their taking a position.
- State your position clearly. Focus on simple and vivid examples. Emphasize your credibility/experience/expertise. Ask directly where they stand. Encourage them to express an opinion without judging it.
- Apply gentle pressure. Express your frustration with their neutrality. Ask for their support. State mutual benefits and mutual losses. Try to find a common enemy.
- Tell them, *"Think about it and let me know what it would take to win your support"*. You want to confront them gently, but leave the door open for them to come to you when it's clear where they stand. Make your message lively and interesting. Encourage them to learn. Invite questions and requests for clarification. They are not

worth a lot of your energy. Basically, they will take a position when they feel it's safe to do so.

Adversaries - these are the people who take up much of your emotional energy and time. We complain about them to our friends. We worry about what they will do next. We plot to defeat their efforts. They become huge energy drains for us in our work. In your interactions with your Adversaries, typically, negotiation has not worked. People fall into the categories of Backslappers or Opponents until you have tried unsuccessfully to negotiate some trust in the relationship or a plan of agreed action. People become Adversaries only when your attempts at negotiating agreement and trust have failed. The problem is that many times we wrongly identify others as Adversaries based on very little information.

☼   Skill Builders for Use with Adversaries:

- The first step in dealing with Adversaries is to find out if they indeed deserve that title. The only way to do that is in direct conversation with them.
- Adversaries are going to pursue their own vision. And since they are people you have no trust in, you are in the absolute worst position to exert influence over them.
- The solution is to let go. Stop trying to persuade them and stop investing energy into trying to undermine or destroy them.
- The general strategy is to deactivate them - to get them to stop working actively against you. State your position. Be as clear as you can be about what you are trying to do and why. This represents your final hope that reason and good intentions will be persuasive.
- State in a neutral way your best understanding of their position. One goal with an Adversary is to defuse the situation. One way to do that is to communicate understanding of (not agreement with) their position. Talk about their concerns ("I've done my homework on this ...") and be alert for any signs of a win-win situation. Use experts or authorities your Adversary will recognize and will respect. Adversaries are not interested in why

you're convinced. They want to know why *they* should be.

- Identify your own contribution to the problem. Whatever damage the Adversary can do to you has already been done. Manipulative strategies can only thrive in darkness, so shine a light on everything that you are aware of in regard to the relationship. This is an implied commitment on your part to cease your side of the hostilities. This may not win the support of the Adversary, but it makes it easier for bystanders and third parties to take your side. This is an example of a healthy operating style.
- End the conversation with your plans and make no further demands on them.

4. Being the Center of a Knowledge Network

Key contributors understand that information is power. They are skilled at forming alliances that put them in the know. In effect, they work to place themselves at the center of organizational knowledge - wherever, and with whomever, that knowledge resides. When people are connected in this way, their knowledge is leveraged. Drill down into the center of the networks you have formed, and you're likely to hit a gusher of collective brainpower. It's a knowledge economy from now on, driven by the power of ideas and accumulated knowledge. What has occurred in recent years is the next evolutionary step of knowing people. That means having access to networks of people who know those you know. Thanks to the Internet, hundreds of thousands of common-interest-based networks have formed via e-mail lists, blogs, and newsgroups, so all you really have to do is to be a part of five or ten key networks and it's like having access to thousands of potential sources of knowledge. If you belong to the right networks, you can gain immediate access to other networks. You evolve faster and with less stress. You become part of a flow. Networks provide that flow.

Skill Builders:

☼　　Associate yourself with the centers of influence. Hang with 'movers and shakers'. Associate with others who are also successful and influential, including those in other industries.

5. Continuous Résumé-ing

Key contributors know that they can't afford to become *'R.O.A.D.- kill'*: **R**etired **O**n **A**ctive **D**uty.

When businesses inevitably change, the question becomes: *How can we, as individuals, contribute in ways that make us indispensable AND help our company survive?*. It doesn't take long for knowledge and skills to become outdated in today's world. Technological advances and the flood of new information make it hard to even keep up with what's going on. College graduates can find even their most advanced technical skills outdated in a matter of years. Some careers don't even get a chance to change - they simply disappear. Don't let yourself stagnate on the job. Job security is gone in the new organization. In today's business environment, where fewer people have to do much more with much less, you have to create your own opportunities. The driving force of your career must come from you, not from the organization. The age of 'free agentry' is upon us. This means working formally or informally under contract, always with an eye to your personal value in the marketplace. The key is doing things intensely, developing those skills professionally that will allow you to grow, developing a uniqueness, and expanding your skills. Who is ultimately responsible for making your work life and your career as effective as it can be?　Not your boss, not your colleagues - *you* are.

James Citrin and Richard Smith, in their book *The Five Patterns of Extraordinary Careers*,[72] have recognized a pattern in extraordinarily successful individuals. They point out that life-altering moments occur in careers in much the same way as they do in nature.

The primary sources shaping the *Grand Canyon* are not centuries of steady erosion (contrary to what many people assume), but earthshaking mudflows known as 'lahars'. These geologic events occur infrequently as massive flash flooding sends tons of boulders cascading down. A single lahar can reshape the landscape more dramatically than hundreds of years of steady erosion. The constant flow of water over the countryside does reshape the path of rivers and form valleys, but *Grand Canyons* are usually the result of grand events.

Careers are similar. Like the river flowing continually over time, steady access to new experiences, met with strong performances, are required to keep your career on an upward trajectory. But there will likely be a limited number of lahar opportunities in your working life - events that, if taken advantage of, will positively and dramatically change your career's direction. Key contributors learn to identify and gain access to these intermittent events and use them to their advantage. They employ numerous creative strategies and all the resources at their disposal to gain experiences required for an extraordinary career. Part of the trick involves identifying valuable opportunities that others may not see. It is natural and comfortable to be drawn toward the places in organizations that are successful and running smoothly. But this may not be the best strategy for success in the workplace. The most significant opportunities may be found in the most distressed parts of the organization. Often the best you can do in an already successful situation is to maintain the status quo. In a distressed or untested unit or company, however, the expectations can be much lower, but the potential to generate a positive impact can be much greater. The parts of the organization that cause the most pain are also often the most highly visible. Fix them, and management will sit up and take notice.

Skill Builders:

☼   Practice *kaizen* [73] - the art of continuous improvement, the relentless quest for the better way, for higher quality craftsmanship, the daily pursuit of perfection. Kaizen keeps you reaching, stretching to outdo yesterday. Enough of those small incremental gains will add up to a valuable competitive advantage. Don't rest on your laurels. 'Good' today is just 'so-so' tomorrow. Every employee is responsible for continually upgrading their job performance. Your productivity, response time, quality, cost control, and customer service should all show steady gains. And your skills should be in a state of constant renewal.

☼   Homework - studying on your own - should become a regular part of your weekly routine. Read, attend workshops and seminars, take courses, volunteer for understudy or apprenticeship assignments that let you learn from experts. Accept lateral moves that will broaden you. Ask for learning opportunities. You need specialized knowledge, but you also need to know how your field or profession is changing. Delve deeper. Develop transferable skills that give 'portability' to your career. The more you know how to do, and the better you do it, the more valuable you become. Defend your career by developing a better package of knowledge and skills than the next person.

☼   Discover your strengths through 'feedback analysis'. Here are some steps for performing such a self-analysis:
- Whenever you make a key decision or take part in a key action, write down what you expect will happen.
- Nine or 12 months later, compare the actual results with your expectations.
- Practiced consistently, this simple method will allow you, within a fairly short period of time, to determine exactly where your strengths lie. It will also show you what you are doing or failing to do that deprives you of the full benefit of your strengths. It will show you where you are not particularly competent.
- First, concentrate on your strengths - put yourself where your strengths can produce results.
- Second, work on improving your strengths. You will have seen where you need to improve your skills or acquire new ones. You will find gaps in your knowledge.
- Third, discover where your intellectual arrogance is causing disabling ignorance and overcome it.

Remedy your bad habits: the things you do or fail to do that inhibit your effectiveness and performance.

- Focus on your strengths. Waste as little effort as possible on improving areas of low competence. It takes far more energy and work to improve from incompetence to mediocrity than it does to improve from first-rate performance to excellence. Often we choose to spend our time and energy trying to turn incompetent performance into mediocre performance. Your energy, resources, and time should go instead to making your areas of competent performance into star-power.

Others' Opinions Grant You the Gift of Knowledge

Don't fool yourself into thinking the opinions of others don't matter, especially the opinions of those critical few on whom your work depends. In the interdependent workplace, these critical few are often your internal customers and suppliers as well as your boss and your colleagues. Your credibility and reputation play a key role in how far and how quickly you move ahead. Soliciting input from others always leaves you with a clearer view of your blind spots.

☼   Get a good 360-degree look at your skillsets. Sit down with an experienced facilitator to go over your strengths and areas for development and get a plan.

- What are my greatest strengths?
- Which of my skills are most valuable to the organization? Where can I add value to the organization? (It may not be in the job you have now).
- How have I demonstrated my value lately?
- Who among my customers can attest to what I have done well?
- What evidence is there that my skills are state of the art?
- What do I need to learn to be more effective?
- Who do I need to know outside the company to enhance my effectiveness?
- Will my year-end resume look different than last year's?

☼   Don't insulate yourself. Becoming defensive and hostile when faced with constructive criticism (or not seeking it out at all) will leave you insulated from the truth and greatly limit your potential.

☼   Ask your employees how you could be doing better. Worried they won't be honest with you? Find a way to ask in a nonthreatening and inviting, open-ended manner: "I'm really trying to improve in the area of giving clear directives.

Have you seen any ways that I could do better at this in the projects we work on together"?

☼ Go to all the people with whom you interact on a regular basis and ask them what you need to be doing to be more effective in your job.
  - Ask what they consider to be 'critically important'.
  - Ask: *"What do you need from me to be more effective"?*
  - Set up regular meetings with your boss and ask how you are doing, and make clear what contributions you are making. Give your boss data that are couched in the manner of improving your performance: what you need to be more effective, or how best to use your talents.
  - Be proactive about clarifying miscommunication or misunderstanding.

Expand Your Skills and Become Indispensable

Examine your job and identify the critical few make-or-break factors important for job success and set about embracing them. Continuing to focus only on 'doing what you do best' might be one of the worst things you could do. Succeeding in business is not politics, maneuvering, and backstabbing. Those things get people in trouble eventually. What has staying power is performing and problem-solving on your current job, having some notable strengths, and seeking new tasks you don't yet know how to do.

Δ Stay current. Keep abreast of the current business literature, but consider branching out and delving into other areas that, while they may not be directly related, may provide some other types of useful information.

☼ Continually update your *résumé* - not the one on paper, but your actual skills. Find the 'hot' new area and become your company's expert.

Δ   Read more broadly. Tune in to 'hot-topic' periodicals, blogs and channels. Scan these regularly for trends, relevant issues, knowledge, and general business savvy.

Δ   Talk with the people in your organization and others who know about the business. Do lunch or just stop by to chat.

Δ   Get close to customers. Customer service is the best place to get to know about your business.

Δ   Learn to think like an expert in your business thinks. Take problems to internal experts and business consultants and ask them, "What are the keys you look for"? Observe what they consider significant.

☼   Get and use a 'career board of directors'. Select some highfliers who know the business well and ask for their guidance in advancing your career. They will be flattered and will take a new interest in you and in making sure their guidance pays off.

☼   Break out of your career comfort zone. Take a course, in a new area, task, or trade. Volunteer for task forces and projects that are multi-functional and multi-business in nature.

☼   Build a performance track record of variety. Start things up, fix things, innovate, make plans, come in under budget. Focus on activities that are at the core of what your organization does. Find a business opportunity and make a reasoned case for it. Pick a big problem and work maniacally at it.

Chapter Five

Boundary Spanning: Get On The Horizontal Fast Track

"Never doubt that a small group of thoughtful, committed citizens can change the world.
Indeed, it's the only thing that ever has".

                                                                    - Margaret Meade

Organizational Cross-Pollination

If visibility is a function of other people knowing *you*, *Boundary Spanning* is a function of *you knowing other people* - and the *right* people. The skills associated with boundary spanning are important both to individual contribution in the organization and to making the organization function most effectively.

In days past, organizational security came from being in the center of an organization, not taking chances, and not rocking the boat. Now organizational security comes from being at the edges - where the organization needs to relate to other groups. Key contributors communicate across functional boundaries, influence one side for another, broker information, mediate differences along the edges where the organization needs coordinated learning.

The new organizational concept of '*boundaryless-ness*' involves breaking down all the barriers that divide employees: hierarchy, job function, geography. The key to the skill is '*lateral learning*' - finding out what your colleagues are doing right and carrying those practices into your own organization. This mind-set is critical. If you don't cross-pollinate, you become obsolete.

The implications are staggering. The era of the technology expert - one who has in-depth knowledge of one process or one job - is fading and giving way to an expertise that lies in *breadth* of experience. Today power rests with those who can mine the expertise that lies hidden in veins all across the organization.

Our clients who are job placement specialists tell us that companies now give preference to job seekers with a broad range of experiences, who have not confined themselves to one particular job, one company, or even one industry. In today's leaner organization, individuals are required to be familiar with many different jobs and to be able to manage functions in which they have little or no technical expertise. Individuals on the make in business had better concentrate on acquiring a wide variety of transferable skills, not esoteric skills, as a way to make themselves indispensable. The more you gain experience with the diverse parts of the organization, the more possible it is to see the big picture, both in terms of its possibilities and potentials, and in terms of dysfunction, which might serve to stifle effectiveness.[67]

What Our Surveys Showed

When we analyzed the content of our surveys with organizational key contributors and the managers who hired them, over 54% of those surveyed mentioned some aspect of what we have come to call *'Boundary Spanning'*. Those individuals identified as key contributors displayed one or both of these skills:

1. Being a Connector of People
2. Having a Broad-Based Knowledge of the Workings of the Organization

---

It's a Small World After All

About 50 years ago, *Harvard University* psychologist Stanley Milgram reported the results of a series of studies he labeled *'The Small World Problem'*. [74] He was interested in studying social connectivity. In one study, he obtained at random the names of 160 people who lived in Omaha, Nebraska. Each of these 'participants' was given a packet that detailed the study's purpose and contained the name and address of a stockbroker who worked in Boston and lived in Sharon, Massachusetts. Participants were instructed to place their own name on a roster in the packet and then to mail or deliver

---

212

the packet to someone who they knew personally that might get the packet closer to the Boston stockbroker. They could not mail the packet directly to the target (unless, of course, they knew him personally). Rather, they had to use a strategy of going through someone they did know personally - on a first-name basis. You might deliver the packet to a stockbroker friend, for example, or to an old college roommate, or an aunt who lived in the Boston area. By counting the number of names that appeared on the roster, Milgram could calculate the average number of steps it took to connect to the target (the stockbroker). Most of the packets reached the stockbroker in five or six steps - hence, our fascination with 'six degrees of separation'.

But the most interesting finding of the study proved to be that not all degrees were equal. A total of 64 letters eventually reached the stockbroker. Twenty-four letters reached the stockbroker at his home in Sharon. Of those, 16 were given to him by the same person - a clothing merchant. Of the remaining 40 letters, which reached him at his office, more than half were delivered by two other specific men. In all, half of the responses that came back to the stockbroker were delivered to him by these same three specific people. Six degrees of separation doesn't mean that everyone is linked to everyone else in just six steps. It means that a very small number of people are linked to everyone else in a few steps. The rest of us are linked to the world through these special few.

1. Being a Connector of People

"The person with his finger on the trigger is more powerful than the person who owns the gun".   -
Anonymous

Key contributors have taken the time to network both inside and outside the organization and to gather relationships with those who have the capacity to help. They have nurtured connections with people in other departments, other offices, and other organizations. They form alliances and lateral relationships that eventually become crucial in situations where people need to share different kinds of expertise. The skill is in being able to bring diverse and eclectic groups together and often leading from the middle of the pack to access critical information and to create new combinations and multidisciplinary solutions.

These contributors are extroverted, outgoing, sociable and gregarious, and they develop friendships easily. They are known for their willingness to listen to what others have to say. They have a wealth of social contacts and can be very persuasive in obtaining the assistance of others when needed. Likewise, they are always willing to help others, and they gain goodwill through forming reciprocal relationships. They nurture connections - communicating with people in other departments, at different satellite offices, and even in other organizations. They can use their personal influence behind the scenes, when necessary, to get things done.

The following quotes about our key contributors are typical and are drawn directly from our surveys:

> "He has an extensive network of contacts that provides whatever information or services his unit needs".

> "He really seems to understand that in our industry information is power. He has huge information networks both inside and outside the company. He is successful primarily because of the diversity of input he can obtain from others".

> "A major part of her effectiveness is that she links people and resources and keeps everybody well-informed".

> "He is like his organization's roving ambassador, serving as the eyes and ears for his group in the wider organization".

> "He can handle most technical questions himself, and when he can't, he knows who else in the informal network - regardless of functional area - has the relevant expertise".

"He is skillful at forming alliances and lateral relationships outside his functional area".

Six Degrees of Kevin Bacon

It's not only the *number* of people you know, but the *types of relationships* that are important. In the popular parlor game *Six Degrees of Kevin Bacon*, players are challenged to pick the name of any actor at random and connect him, through movies that he has acted in, to the actor Kevin Bacon. For, example, let's say the actor picked is Val Kilmer. Kilmer never played in a move with Bacon. But he did appear in *Top Gun* with Tom Cruise, and Tom Cruise appeared in *A Few Good Men* with Bacon. Therefore Val Kilmer is connected to Kevin Bacon by two degrees of separation.

Brett Tjaden, a computer scientist at the *University of Virginia,* created a computer program that used the *Internet Movie Database* of 800,000 or so actors and actresses who have ever appeared in a motion picture or television film. The program was able to determine which actor or actress had the lowest 'connection number' - meaning the actor or actress who is connected in the fewest average number of steps to every other actor or actress. That person would be the theoretical 'center of the Hollywood universe'. The most connected actor in history is, in fact, not Kevin Bacon, but Rod Steiger. One might have guessed John Wayne or some other actor who appeared in lots of films. But John Wayne's films were basically all of the same genre: action movies or Westerns. So his connections were limited to actors or actresses who also played in such films. Rod Steiger, on the other hand, made great movies and 'B movies' that went straight to video. He's been in a huge variety of films: comedies, tragedies, action films, Westerns, documentaries, horror movies, and thrillers. He is the most connected actor in history because he has been able to move back and forth among all the different worlds, subcultures, niches, and levels the acting profession has to offer.[75]

Rod Steiger may not exactly be a household name, and he certainly does not have the box-office draw of a Tom Cruise, for example. But that's not the point here. Simply being 'connected' is a major

---

asset in itself. The better connected you are, the more opportunities you have for good things to come your way as they do most often…through other people. For most of us - those of us who depend on other people in our personal and working lives - the more connectivity we have, the better off we are. The implications for the key organization contributor who seeks the skill of boundary spanning are obvious.

Communities of Practice

Key Contributors with the skill of boundary spanning are likely to be members of various *'communities of practice'*. Communities of practice are informal groups whose members regularly engage in sharing and learning, based on a common interest. These types of groups came into existence when individuals interested in a common work-related area, or in an avocation, found it helpful to share what they knew and to learn from others. Professional associations, groups of software developers, and skilled-craft guilds are examples of work-related communities of practice. In the past few years, e-mail, electronic discussion groups, and Internet chat rooms have facilitated the development of communities of practice whose members are not all co-located.

Because we are connected now as never before, in webs of communication and information sharing through the Internet and other media, for the first time we have the capacity for engaging in connected global conversations and coordinated action regarding problems we face and opportunities we detect. These communities of practice have become the engines for the development of social capital. Recent research from the *IBM Institute for Knowledge Management* [76] has shown a number of different mechanisms by which communities of practice influence business outcomes. These include:

- Decreasing the learning curve of new employees
- Responding more rapidly to customer needs and inquiries
- Reducing rework and preventing 'reinvention of the wheel'

- Spawning new ideas for products and services

Boundary spanners have some instinct that helps them relate to the people they meet. Their ability to span many different worlds is likely a function of something intrinsic to their personality: some combination of curiosity, self-confidence, sociability, and energy. But the important thing is that they take the steps necessary to connect themselves to knowledgeable people who have wide-ranging experience, expertise, and worldviews.

2. Having a Broad-Based Knowledge of the Workings of the Organization

"The kind of people I look for to fill the top spots are the eager beavers, the mavericks. These are the ones who try to do more than they're expected to do - they're always reaching".

- Lee Iacocca

Contributors function as roving ambassadors, serving as their group's eyes and ears in the larger organization. They have taken the time to understand the 'big picture' and how various parts of the organization fit together and are interdependent in work output. They 'stay in school' and continue to learn the intricacies and the workings of the organization. In the old days, at the management level, this was referred to as 'managing by walking around'. These mangers knew how the organization and their subordinates worked because they had seen it firsthand.

Key contributors listen across different parts of the organization for what information needs to be understood, communicated, or translated. They explore outside the boundaries of the formal organization and then translate those findings to fit the unique needs of their enterprise. They can elicit the cooperation of those around them by explaining the rationale and providing the 'big picture'. They are skilled at helping others to visualize how the pieces of the organization fit together. They are considered credible sources of organizational information. Most importantly, they seek out work assignments that provide them with the opportunity to see a broader perspective of the organization. When the time comes, they can play

217

a critical role in situations where people need to share different kinds of expertise - establishing strategic alliances or developing new products.

The following quotes about contributors are typical and are drawn directly from our surveys:

> "She knows who can provide critical information or expertise that the entire organization draws on to get work done".

> "He is like a point man, gathering information for and disseminating information about his group in the wider organization".

> "A major part of her effectiveness is that she links people and resources and keeps everybody well-informed".

> "He really seems to understand that in our industry information is power. He has huge information networks both inside and outside the company".

> "He is successful because of the diversity of input he can obtain from others".

> "He can see how the pieces of the larger organizational puzzle fit together".

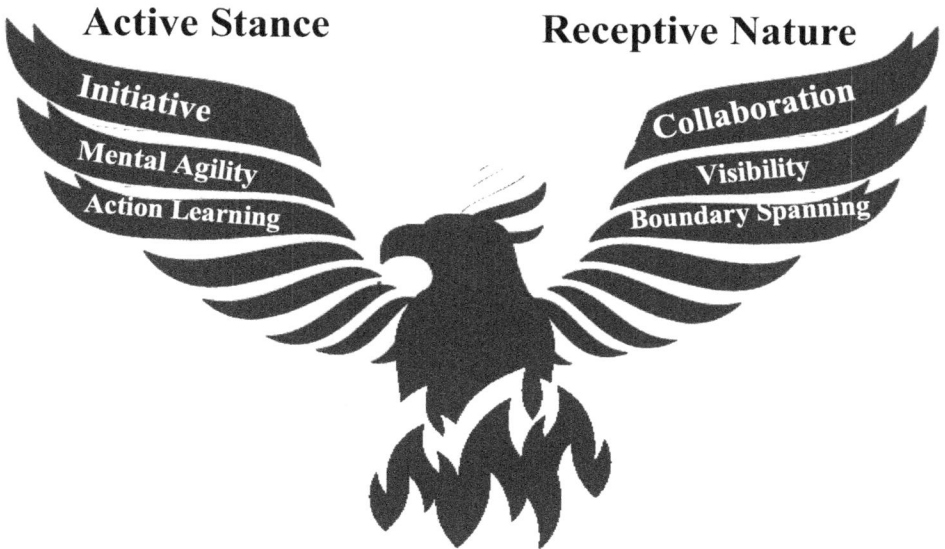

Active Stance

Initiative

Mental Agility

Action Learning

Receptive Nature

Collaboration

Visibility

Boundary Spanning

Are You An Organizational Cross-Pollinator?

It's time to test your '*Boundary Spanning*'. Do you make use of this important strategy? Take this short quiz and find out. For each set of descriptors, those on the right of the page and those on the left, check the ones that apply to you. Check as many items as are descriptive of your work style. Your task here is to make as honest an assessment of your skills as possible. The results will help you to understand how natural this ability is for you and, if you choose, the next section of this chapter will guide you to activities and exercises designed to develop the survival skill of boundary spanning.

☐	I prefer to keep important organizational information I have to myself so as to preserve my competitive advantage.	☐	I seek to share information with others at all levels.
☐	I tend to defer to others to handle the more sensitive or critical organizational issues.	☐	I am often able to use my personal influence behind the scenes to get difficult organizational tasks done.
☐	I am close primarily with only those in my own work group.	☐	I have contacts and a working relationship with a wide variety of people in all parts of the organization.
☐	I tend to keep to myself and concentrate on getting my assigned work done.	☐	I am outgoing and socially gregarious, and I develop friendships easily.
☐	I prefer not to interact much with those at higher organizational levels.	☐	I am confident in my ability and comfortable interacting with people at all organizational levels.
☐	I only have a few people that I trust to provide me with the information I need to do my job.	☐	I am open to input from a wide variety of people and am willing to consider and act on that input
☐	I am well-known within my own work group.	☐	I nurture connections and open communication channels with people in other departments.
☐	My knowledge base is centered on my particular work area.	☐	I know the people who can provide critical information or expertise that the entire network draws on to get work done.
☐	I am most concerned with making sure my department has the information it needs to compete successfully.	☐	I strive to do business with a wide variety of individuals throughout the organization and to keep the communication channels open.

☐ I am known primarily within my own department and not widely known in the organization.	☐ I am one of the people in the organization that everyone seems to talk to the most.
☐ I am focused primarily on getting the work of my department done.	☐ I am interested in understanding how the work of others fits in with the work my department does
☐ I concentrate primarily on knowing how my part of the organization functions.	☐ I try to understand the "big picture" and learn as much as I can about the workings of the larger organization.
☐ I usually look to others when critical information or action is needed.	☐ I am considered the "go-to" person when critical information or action is needed
☐ I am most knowledgeable about the workings of my own area. If information is needed from people in other functional areas, I let other people handle that.	☐ I can handle most technical questions myself, and when I can't, I know who to go to in the organization to get the information I need.
☐ I let those higher up in the organization worry about how to coordinate the work of the various departments.	☐ I have learned about the workings of the organization and am considered a walking compendium of important information.
☐ If someone needs information about my particular area, I can usually find it.	☐ I am considered to be one who can provide critical information or expertise that the entire organization draws on to get things done.
☐ I enjoy work assignments that relate specifically to my area of expertise.	☐ I seek work assignments that provide me with the opportunity to see a broader perspective of the organization.

☐ The job of coordinating how all the pieces of the organization fit together is best handled by those at the top of the organization.	☐ I am skilled at helping others to visualize how the pieces of the puzzle fit together; I have an understanding of the whole of the organization or process.
☐ I know very well how my specific work area functions, but I'm not too informed about the workings of all the other areas of the company.	☐ There have been occasions where I have participated in coming up with innovative and creative solutions to broader organizational problems by using the insights of a wide variety of organizational members.
☐ I'm less comfortable worrying about how the larger organization functions and prefer to focus on my area of responsibility.	☐ I believe it's important to understand the organization system as a whole, with all its complex interactions among the different parts of the company
– _____ **Total Boxes Checked**	**+** _____ **Total Boxes Checked**

Our survey results indicate that over 54% of respondents mentioned some aspect of what we have come to call *'Boundary Spanning'*. Recall that our respondents were either key organization contributors themselves or managers who had the task of selecting employees who would be most valuable to their organization. They occupied all levels of the organization, from executives to individual contributors. In every case, respondents were asked to comment on those skills that they believed made employees indispensable to their companies.

Add the numbers in the Totals boxes together, retaining their arithmetic sign. If your score is between -20 and -10, your boundary spanning ability is underdeveloped. You may be hampered by a tendency to stick only to your own narrow area of interest or ability - a significant handicap in a change-dominant and increasingly global organizational culture. Your boundary spanning skills would be increased by attending to and practicing the exercises and activities in the next section of this chapter

If your total score is between +10 and +20, it is likely that your boundary spanning ability is serving you well. Nevertheless, you may wish to review the exercises and activities in the next section of this chapter to assist you in further developing these skills.

Become an Organizational Ambassador

Recall that boundary spanning is a function of *you knowing other people* - and the *right* people. Likewise, key contributors understand that, in matters of complex problems and constant change, *no one of us is as smart as all of us.* They listen across different parts of their own organization for what information needs to be understood, communicated, or translated. They explore outside the boundaries of the formal organization as well, and then translate those findings and revelations to fit the unique needs of their enterprise. Key contributors know that increasingly it's through informal networks, not just through traditional organizational hierarchy, that information is found and work gets done. These same personal networks can be powerful political tools as well, useful for lining up allies to push initiatives ahead and gathering important information that puts you a step ahead of the competition.

This is a set of skills that is learnable by everyone. If you want to add to your capability in the area of boundary spanning, here are some tips to help you sharpen this capacity.

As you read through the Skill Builders associated with each aspect of Boundary Spanning, circle the symbol beside those you would like to implement as part of your *Key Contributor Ready Kit.* Then use Table 7 in the Appendix to fill out aspects of your *'Boundary Spanning Kit'.*

1. Being a Connector of People

Organization contributors with the skill of boundary spanning take the time to network both inside and outside their organization and to gather access to, and relationships with, those who have the capacity to help. They nurture connections with people in other departments, in offices in other locations, and even in other organizations. They form alliances and lateral relationships that become crucial in situations where people need to share different kinds of expertise across the organization.

In the past, being on the periphery of an organization was early career death. These days, if you're on the edges of the organization, chances are you'll have the opportunity to participate in some meaningful innovation. The reason is simple. In many companies, headquarters is the stronghold of the status quo. The closer you get to the center, the less chance you have to try new things. On the periphery - the boundaries between functions or between the organization and the marketplace - experimentation can take place. This is where new ideas are born, take shape, and are refined. If the ideas work, they can always be 'kicked upstairs'. If they fail, they can be given a quiet burial, and no one will ever know. While you're gathering the information that will put you in the know, make sure you gather information from those with dirty hands: the frontline workers and the customer reps.

Map Your Networks and Build Social Capital[7]

By analyzing your social networks, you can learn how to build better and more effective business relationships, expanding your contacts and broadening your access to organizational expertise. The idea here is to make your information networks as broad and diverse as possible. The more information you have, from a variety of different viewpoints, the better your understanding of the total organization.

Skill Builders:

☼ Map your information networks. Take a look at where your information comes from.
- Is it coming solely from people above you in the organizational hierarchy?
- Is it coming solely from those subordinate to you?
- Are you missing feedback from people with different perspectives?
- Can you seek out, as information sources, people in other functional areas and make them a part of your social network?
- Are your personal networks the result only of the interactions that are built into your schedule (such as planned meetings), rather than ad hoc encounters in the hallways?
- The more narrow and homogenous your social networks are, the less exposure you will have to new concepts and new information. Work to develop a wide base of credible information sources, and you will broaden your organizational awareness.

☼ Can you map a similar network of 'trust' relationships? (Who do you trust in the organization to keep your best interests in mind?)

☼ How about a network map of 'organization energy'? (When you interact with these people, how does it affect your energy level? Are you energized and enlivened? Or do you feel drained and depressed?)

☼ Can you create your network map of 'advisors'? (To whom do you turn for advice before making important decisions?)

☼ How about mapping a network of 'power' or 'influence' in your organization?

☼ How about mapping an 'innovation' network? (With whom are you most likely to discuss a new idea?)

Δ   Look to the edges where your organization connects with other organizations and with the community at large. Look to the boundaries of mature markets, the geographic fringes, and emerging markets. Educate yourself in these areas and connect with the movers and shakers there.

☼   Nurture relationships in which you have under-invested. Decrease your reliance on relationships you have over-invested in, and you will strengthen your personal networks in a way that will pay big dividends.

⊍   The luck literature references the notion of *'destiny pairing'*[77]. If a person walks into your business life - someone with whom you feel a quick, strong positive reaction, don't let that person get away. This is often someone who is different from just a friend. Rather this is a business connection who could change the course of your career and the nature of your luck.

Venture Outside the Boundaries of Your Organization

Many organizations cling to the outdated notion that as long as they indirectly create the right context - more off-sites, more company picnics, and more coffee machines in the hallways - informal networks will flourish. That is simply not enough. Social networks cannot be aligned with organizational goals through those kinds of random interventions. As organizations grow in size, geographical scope, and complexity, 'communities of practice' become ever more important as a method of improving organizational performance.

The savvy organization contributor is likely to be a member of one of more of these communities. These communities are often the engines for the development of social capital. Interaction here leads to knowledge sharing, which in turn positively influences the business performance of all the members within their respective organizations.

Skill Builders:

Δ   What 'communities of practice' can you join or work to form? Communities of practice:

- have the potential to overcome inherent problems of a slow-moving traditional hierarchy in a fast-moving virtual economy.
- quickly transfer the knowledge necessary to address customer issues, especially when the expertise needed to solve a particular client problem may be separated by time zones, distance, or organizational boundaries.
- are effective ways for organizations to handle unstructured problems and to share knowledge outside the traditional structural boundaries.
- reduce rework and prevent 'reinvention of the wheel', allowing members to more easily reuse existing knowledge.
- decrease the learning curve of new employees (rapidly increasing their productivity).
- readily identify subject matter experts who can answer questions and guide members to resources.
- create mentor-student relationships between more junior members of a profession and more established practitioners.
- help individuals gain a broader perspective of their roles within the organization.
- are useful vehicles for creating shared narratives (myths, stories, and metaphors) that can transfer tacit knowledge and maintain long-term organizational memory.
- spawn new ideas for products and services and serve as breeding grounds for innovation.

Get beyond your *'home clump'* [78]. Those who study social networking suggest that the average person has about 300 *'weak ties'* - individuals whom we know well enough to call by name and have a conversation with. If each of them has

300 connections, that brings our second tier network to 90,000 individuals, and our tertiary links to 27,000,000 people. Witness the strength of weak ties in expanding our boundaries.

2. Having a Broad-Based Knowledge of the Workings of the Organization

Key organization contributors with the skill of boundary spanning function as roving ambassadors - serving as their group's eyes and ears in the larger organization. They take the time to understand the 'big picture', how various parts of the organization fit together and are interdependent. They 'stay in school' and continue to learn the intricacies of the workings of the organization.

Skill Builders:

Δ   When you meet someone at work, find out what he or she does and how it connects to your area. Know who in your organization does work that connects to yours, either as a provider or as a customer. Make it a point to develop a good relationship with them.

☼   'Stay in school' in your organization. Learn by walking around.

☼   Seek out job assignments that give you the bigger picture of how the organization works – '*the 35,000-foot view*'.

The Way Forward

The model we have built deals in 'prevailing orientation' and 'key contributor skills'. Some of these attributes appear deeply rooted in personal style, almost automatic in nature. But we believe each of these qualities has definite learnable components. The value of model building lies in its application. If you want to stand out from the crowd and be a significant contributor to your organization, this model tells you how.

Focus on Your Strengths, Not Your Weaknesses

From childhood, we are taught to focus on improving in areas of perceived weakness rather than building on our strengths. We work hard at fixing what is wrong or overcoming our deficits, rather than capitalizing on our talents. So now you have the luxury of taking a different track. First, give some thought to those times at work when you felt 'in the flow' - even though you were probably working hard. Remember? Time flew by, and you were totally absorbed in what you were doing. This is the deeply satisfying stuff and probably some of the best work experiences you have ever had. Those were the times when you were operating from your strengths. Wouldn't it be great if you could find (or create) a work environment where you could use those strengths? Well, you can and we're about to help you plan out how to do just that.

Consider this statistic: According to a 10-year *Gallup* survey of more than 10 million people on the topic of positive and engaged people at work, only one-third of employees believe they have the opportunity to do what they do best every day.[79] Sadly, they are missing out on the power of being engaged, contributing, and effective. Imagine the dramatic improvement in productivity and commitment that you could achieve if you could start focusing on what you do best. According to *Gallup*, when people are given the opportunity to engage in work that uses their strengths, they are six times as likely to report having an excellent quality of life at work.

The belief that we can best improve by focusing on weakness, although deeply entrenched in our work culture, flies in the face of research. In fact, it takes far more energy and work to improve from incompetence to mediocrity than it does to improve from first-rate performance to excellence. Too often we choose to spend our time and energy trying to turn lackluster performance into mediocre performance. Your energy, resources, and time should go instead to making your areas of competent performance into star-power. The new organization requires that we sharpen our best skills, focusing not on our deficits but on our strengths.

We know that a focus on 'developmental' issues results in 'incremental' change - serving only to get you back on track - the same track you have been on.

A focus on your strengths can well result in 'transformational' change, multiplying your impact and moving you in the direction of high performance.

So, work on your identified development needs for sure - you want *all* your contributor skills in place. You never know when you'll need them. But put the bulk of your efforts toward transforming your strengths into extraordinary accomplishment.

Think about which parts of a project you would naturally gravitate to or where you feel your strengths lie. Make some notes for yourself. Capture what you have learned about yourself in terms of when you are the most engaged. You're going to build your career around these peak moments.

Take a look back at the surveys you have taken in each previous chapter, which measure your 'prevailing orientations' and 'key contributor skills'.

Which of the two 'prevailing orientations' did you most frequently endorse? If your initial inclinations were well-balanced, all the better. But you are going to capitalize on whatever you discovered was your strongest prevailing orientation. Which specific elements did you most closely identify with?

Now have a look at the surveys you filled out in each chapter. Which among the four skillsets represents your greatest strengths? You may (and probably do) have more than one 'key contributor skill' strength. Look back carefully at how you filled out each survey. You will likely be able to tease out which of the specific elements of those skillsets were your strongest suits.

In the skillset of mental agility, for example, are you primarily quick in thought and action or are you creative with a thirst for innovation? Do you find that you have a strong intuitive skill? Are you skillful at taking calculated risks?

Is your action learning skillset well developed? Do you make it a habit to take the time to observe the critical elements of *how* the organization works (not just what it routinely accomplishes)? Are you skillful at helping others to learn from your group's experience? Can you help your colleagues see how to integrate this learning and apply it to other organizational issues?

In the area of visibility, are you the one in your organization who is well-known by most everyone? Do you have a unique reputation for competence? Are you skillful at communicating your ideas all across the organization, not just in your technical field? Are you well connected to the people who have critical organizational knowledge? Are you working to update your skills in the hottest technical areas?

When it comes to boundary spanning, do you have a good working knowledge of the entire organization? Do you know how your function connects to the rest of the enterprise? Do you use your personal connections to put the right people together for collaborative knowledge sharing?

Drill down into each of your strongest skillsets. See if you can identify those micro-skills that set you apart from all the rest of humanity and that will provide your springboard for becoming a *Key Contributor* in your organization.

Donald J. Minnick Ph. D.

Appendix

A Plan for Stocking Your *Key Contributor Ready Kit*

Table 1: Your Key Contributor Profile

How to Use Your Scores: Review your scores on the self-rating scales that appear with each chapter. Enter your scores in the table to map your strengths and any threats you might face to your capacity for organizational contribution. Use the table to plan development activities to ensure that you are a key organization contributor.

PREVAILING ORIENTATION			
	For Development (<13 or >17)		Strength (between 13 and 17)
INITIATIVE (pg. 38)			
COLLABORATION (pg. 38)			
KEY CONTRIBUTOR SKILLS			
	For Development (-20 to -10)	Neutral (-9 to +9)	Strength (+10 to +20)
MENTAL AGILITY (pg. 87)			
ACTION LEARNING (pg. 135)			
VISIBILITY (pg. 172)			
BOUNDARY SPANNING (pg. 219)			

Definitions

For Development: Your result on this prevailing orientation or skillset indicates that you are most likely not currently viewed as a 'key contributor' in your organization. Your capacity for organization contribution would be enhanced with some focused developmental effort in this area.

Neutral: Your result on this factor indicates that your capacity for organization contribution fell within the range of the average individual.

Strength: Your result on this prevailing orientation or skillset indicates that your capacity for organization contribution fell within the range of those individuals who are likely to be 'key contributors'. However, you still might want to sharpen your skills in those areas within this domain that you feel are weaknesses for you.

Stocking Your *Key Contributor Ready Kit*

The following tables allow you to add specific Skill Builders for each of the prevailing orientations and skillsets that have been identified in *The Phoenix Factor Model*. Review the results of your self-assessments and use the following tables to put together a plan to become a 'Key Organization Contributor'.

Table 2: Personal Initiative Kit

		PLAN
PREVAILING ORIENTATION		
Initiative		In this table enter those Skill Builders you have chosen in Chapter One to become part of your action plan for organization contribution.
1. Proactivity		
2. An Internal Locus of Control		
3. An Achievement Orientation		
4. Hope and Confidence		

Table 3: Collaboration Kit

		PLAN
PREVAILING ORIENTATION		
Collaboration		In this table enter those Skill Builders you have chosen in Chapter One to become part of your action plan for organization contribution.
1. An Orientation Toward Others		
2. Responsiveness to the Needs of Others		
3. Polished People Skills		

Table 4: Mental Agility Kit

		PLAN
SKILL		
Mental Agility		In this table enter those Skill Builders you have chosen in Chapter Two to become part of your action plan for organization contribution.
1. A Quickness in Thought and Action		
2. A Well-Calibrated Intuitive Skill		
3. A Willingness to Act on Calculated Risks		
4. A Creative Mind-Set and a Thirst for Innovation		

Table 5: Action Learning Kit

		PLAN
SKILL		
Action Learning		In this table enter those Skill Builders you have chosen in Chapter Three to become part of your action plan for organization contribution.
1. Observant Participation		
2. Facilitating Collaborative Meaning		
3. Leveraging Actionable Knowledge		

Table 6: Visibility Kit

		PLAN
SKILL		
Visibility		In this table enter those Skill Builders you have chosen in Chapter Four to become part of your action plan for organization contribution.
1. Being Widely Known in the Organization		
2. Being Known as Competent		
3. Being a Clear Communicator of Ideas		
4. Being the Center of a Knowledge Network		
5. Continuous Résumé-ing		

Table 7: Boundary Spanning Kit

		PLAN
SKILL		
Boundary Spanning		In this table enter those Skill Builders you have chosen in Chapter Five to become part of your action plan for organization contribution.
1. Being a Connector of People		
2. Having a Broad-Based Knowledge of the Workings of the Organization		

Notes

1. https://www.ysc.com

2. Jay Parini, *Promised Land: thirteen books that changed America*, (Doubleday, 2008)

3. Maria Konnikova, *The Biggest Bluff: how I learned to pay attention, master myself, and win*, (Penguin Press, 2020)

4. Julian Rotter, *Social learning and clinical psychology.* (NY: Prentice-Hall, 1954)

5. Max Gunther, *How to Get Lucky: 13 techniques for discovering and taking advantage of life's good breaks,* (Harriman House, 1986)

6. David C. McClelland, "Achievement Orientation Can Be Learned," *Harvard Business Review*, 43 (1965): 6-24.

7. Allan Reiss, Brian Haas, and Debra Mills, "The Role of the Amygdala in Sociability," *Journal of Neuroscience,* 29 (2009): 1132-1139.

8. Max Gunther, *The Luck Factor: Why Some People Are Luckier Than Others and How You Can Become One of Them* (London: Macmillan Publishing Company, Inc., 1997).

9. Ibid.

10. Stacy Collette, "12 Ways to Plump Up Your Paycheck: No. 7 Be a Top Performer at Your Current Employer," www.computerworld.com, November 10, 2008.

11. Baruch Eitan, Ran R. Hassin, and Yaacov Schul. "Non-Conscious Goal Pursuit in Normal Environments: The Use of Implicit Learning," *Psychological Science* 19, no. 3 (2008).

12. Martin E.P. Seligman, *Learned Optimism: How to Change Your Mind and Your Life* (New York: Vintage, 2006).

13. Max Gunther, *The Luck Factor: Why Some People Are Luckier Than Others and How You Can Become One of Them* (London: Macmillan Publishing Company, Inc., 1997).

14. Thomas J. Peters and Robert H. Waterman, *In Search of Excellence: Lessons from America's Best Run Companies* (New York: HarperCollins Publishers, 1982).

15. Larena is a network of researchers funded by the Educational Science Committee (ESC) at the Swedish Research Council and is monitored in cooperation with the National Institute for Working Life, CMTO, University of Linköping, and the Department of Human Work Sciences at Luleå University of Technology, www.larena.se/english_partners.shtml

16. David C. McClelland, "Achievement Orientation Can Be Learned," *Harvard Business Review*, 43 (1965): 6-24.

17. Jerome Groopman, *The Anatomy of Hope: How People Prevail in the Face of Illness* (New York: Random House Trade Paperbacks, 2005).

18. R.S. Feldman. *Development Across the Life Span* (Upper River, NJ: Prentice Hall, 1997).

19. Dettef Fetchenhauer and others, "Solidarity and Prosocial Behavior: An Integration of Social and Psychological Perspectives," in *How to Explain Prosocial and Solidarity Behavior: A Comparison of Framing Theory with Related Meta-Theoretical Paradigms,* ed. Hans Werner Bierhoff (US: Springer, 2006).

20. William Poundstone, *Prisoner's Dilemma* (New York: Doubleday, 1992).

21. Gregory Berns, reported in www.columbiamissourian.com, August 9, 2002.

22. Tiziana Casciaro and Miguel Lobo, "Fool vs. Jerk: Whom Would You Hire?", *Harvard Business Review*, 83 (6) (2005).

23. Kelley, Robert and Caplan, Janet, "How Bell Labs Creates Star Performers," *Harvard Business Review,* July/Aug (1993).

24. www.netfutureinstitute.com.

25. Thomas H. Davenport and John C. Beck, *The Attention Economy: Understanding the New Currency of Business* (Watertown: Harvard Business School Press, 2002).

26. Ibid.

27. Tony Bourdain, *Kitchen Confidential: Adventures in the Culinary Underbelly* (London: Bloomsbury, 2000).

28. James M. Citrin and Richard Smith, *The 5 Patterns of Extraordinary Careers: The Guide to Achieving Success and Satisfaction.* (New York: Three Rivers Press, 2005).

29. Thomas H. Davenport and John C. Beck, *The Attention Economy: Understanding the New Currency of Business.* (Waterbury: Harvard Business School Press, 2002).

30. Diana Hunt and Pam Hait, *The Tao of Time* (Whitby, Ontario, Canada: Fireside, 1991).

31. Malcolm Gladwell, *Blink: The Power of Thinking Without Thinking.* (London: Little, Brown and Company, 2005).

32. Ibid.

33. Gary Klein, *The Power of Intuition: How to Use Your Gut Feelings to Make Better Decisions at Work* (New York: Doubleday, a division of Random House, Inc., 2003).

34. Malcolm Gladwell, *Blink: The Power of Thinking Without Thinking* (London: Little, Brown and Company, 2005).

35. Robert I. Sutton, *Weird Ideas That Work: How to Build a Creative Company* (New   York: Free Press, 2007).

36. Max Gunther, *The Luck Factor: Why Some People Are Luckier Than Others and How You Can Become One of Them* (London: Macmillan Publishing Company, Inc., 1997).

37. Ibid.

38. Ibid.

39. Ibid.

40. Ibid.

41. Ibid.

42. Malcolm Gladwell, *Blink: The Power of Thinking Without Thinking* (New York: Little Brown and Company, 2005).

43. Ibid.

44. Max Gunther, *How to Get Lucky: 13 techniques for discovering and taking advantage of life's good breaks,* (Harriman House, 1986)

45. David Bayles and Ted Orland, *Art and Fear: Observations on the Perils (and Rewards) of Artmaking* (Eugene: Image Continuum Press, 2001).

46. Max Gunther, *How to Get Lucky: 13 techniques for discovering and taking advantage of life's good breaks,* (Harriman House, 1986)

47. Malcolm Gladwell, *Blink: The Power of Thinking Without Thinking* (New York: Little Brown and Company, 2005).

48. Margaret Wheatley, *Leadership and the New Science: Discovering Order in a Chaotic World* (San Francisco: Berrett-Koehler Publishers, 2006).

49. William Poundstone, *How Would You Move Mt. Fuji: Microsoft's Cult of the Puzzle—How the World's Smartest Companies Select the Most Creative Thinkers* (London: Little, Brown and Company, 2004).

50. Kurtzman, Joel, "An Interview with Rosabeth Moss-Kanter," *Strategy + Business,* third quarter, 1999.

51. Richard Wiseman, *The Luck Factor: Four Essential*

Principles (Burbank: Miramax, 2004).

52. Daniel J. Simons and Christopher F. Chabris, "Gorillas in our Midst: Sustained Inattentional Blindness for Dynamic Events," *Perception*, 28 (1999): 1059-74.

53. Alan Webber, *The World Café: Shaping Our Futures Through Conversations That Matter* (San Francisco: Berrett-Koehler Publishers, Inc., 2005).

54. Ronald H. Dukenski, Principal, *Quadrangle Management Consultants, LLC* (personal communication).

55. Max Gunther, *How to Get Lucky: 13 techniques for discovering and taking advantage of life's good breaks,* (Harriman House, 1986)

56. John P. Kotter, *What Leaders Really Do* (Watertown: Harvard Business School Press, 1999).

57. Max Gunther, *The Luck Factor: Why Some People Are Luckier Than Others and How You Can Become One of Them* (London: Macmillan Publishing Company, Inc., 1997).

58. Ibid

59. Mark Granovetter, "The Strength of Weak Ties: A Network Theory Revisited," *Sociological Theory*, 1 (1983).

60. Malcolm Gladwell, *The Tipping Point: How Little Things Can Make a Big Difference* (Newport Beach: Back Bay Books, 2002).

61. Larena is a network of researchers funded by the Educational Science Committee (ESC) at the Swedish Research Council and is monitored in cooperation with the National Institute for Working Life, CMTO, University of Linköping, and the Department of Human Work Sciences at Luleå University of Technology, www.larena.se/english_partners.shtml.

62. Robert Sternberg, *Successful Intelligence: How Practical and Creative Intelligence Determines Success in Life* (New York: Plume, 1997).

63. Malcolm Gladwell, *The Tipping Point: How Little Things Can Make a Big Difference* (Newport Beach: Back Bay Books, 2002).

64. *Holy Bible, New International Version* (Grand Rapids: Zondervan Publishing, 1987).

65. National Research Council, www.nationalacademies.org/nrc/index.htm

66. Max Gunther, *How to Get Lucky: 13 techniques for discovering and taking advantage of life's good breaks,* (Harriman House, 1986)

67. Dean Tjosvold and Barbara Wisse, *Power and Interdependence in Organizations* (Cambridge: Cambridge University Press, 2009).

68. Robert B. Cialdini, *Influence: The Psychology of Persuasion* (New York: Collins Business Publishers, 2006).

69. Thomas J. Peters, *The Pursuit of WOW: Every Person's Guide to Topsy-Turvy Times* (New York: Vintage Publishers, 1994).

70. Peggy Klaus, *Brag: The Art of Tooting Your Own Horn Without Blowing It* (New York: Business Plus, 2004).

71. Peter Block, *The Empowered Manager: Positive Political Skills at Work* (Hoboken:Jossey-Bass, 1991).

72. James M. Citrin and Richard Smith, *The 5 Patterns of Extraordinary Careers: The Guide for Achieving Success and Satisfaction* (New York: Three Rivers Press, 2005).

73. Imai, Masaaki, *Kaizen: the key to Japan's competitive success*, New York: Random House, 1986.

74. Stanley Milgram, "The Small World Problem," *Psychology Today*, 1(1), (1967): 60-

75. Malcolm Gladwell, *The Tipping Point: How Little Things Can Make a Big Difference* (Newport Beach: Back Bay Books, 2002).

76. E.L. Lesser and J. Storck, "Communities of Practice and Organizational Performance," *IBM Systems Journal— Knowledge Management* 40, no. 4 (2001).

77. Max Gunther, *How to Get Lucky: 13 techniques for discovering and taking advantage of life's good breaks,* (Harriman House, 1986)

78. Ibid

79. http://www.gallup.com/consulting/52/Employee-Engagement.aspx.

We'd love to hear your reactions to this work. Contact us at
djmminnick@gmail.com with your comments, your success
stories, or your additions to the thinking represented by the
Phoenix Factor Model.

Made in the USA
Columbia, SC
20 June 2021